Siruthavoor

An Iron Age-Early Historical burial site, Tamil Nadu, South India

Smriti Haricharan

Archaeopress Archaeology

ARCHAEOPRESS PUBLISHING LTD
Gordon House
276 Banbury Road
Oxford OX2 7ED

www.archaeopress.com

ISBN 978 1 78491 435 6
ISBN 978 1 78491 436 3 (e-Pdf)

© Archaeopress and S Haricharan 2016

Cover: Burial 7, urn with capstone

All rights reserved. No part of this book may be reproduced, in any form or
by any means, electronic, mechanical, photocopying or otherwise,
without the prior written permission of the copyright owners.

Printed in England by Oxuniprint, Oxford
This book is available direct from Archaeopress or from our website www.archaeopress.com

Contents

List of Figures iii
List of Tables v
Acknowledgment vii
Preface ix

Chapter 1 Introduction 1
1.1 WHY STUDY THE MEGALITHS IN SOUTH INDIA 1
1.2 USING THE TERM: 'MEGALITHIC' 1
1.3 CHRONOLOGY AND DISTRIBUTION OF MEGALITHIC BURIALS AROUND THE WORLD 2
1.4 THE IRON AGE-EARLY HISTORIC OR 'MEGALITHIC' BURIALS OF INDIA 3
1.5 THE SANGAM LITERATURE AND IA-EH BURIALS OF TAMILNADU 4
1.6 SOCIAL AND ECONOMIC STRUCTURE OF THE IRON AGE-EARLY HISTORICAL PERIOD BASED ON LITERARY SOURCES AND THE ARCHAEOLOGICAL EVIDENCE 4
1.7 ARCHAEOLOGICAL EVIDENCE FROM EXCAVATED SITES 6
1.8 CHRONOLOGY OF TAMIL NADU IA-EH BURIALS 9
1.9 TYPOLOGY OF THE BURIALS 9
1.10 PREVIOUS CLASSIFICATIONS OF MEGALITHIC BURIALS 11
1.11 THE IA-EH SITE-SIRUTHAVOOR 13

Chapter 2 Siruthavoor: An Iron Age-Early Historic site 14
2.1 INTRODUCTION 14
2.2 GEOMORPHOLOGY 15
2.3 GEOLOGY 15
2.4 SOIL TYPES 16
2.5 CLIMATE AND RAINFALL 16
2.6 VEGETATION 16
2.7 THE IA-EH BURIALS OF SIRUTHAVOOR 16

Chapter 3 Methodology 18
3.1 INTRODUCTION 18
3.2 EXPLORATION AND EXCAVATION 18
3.3 CLASSIFICATION AND MAPPING OF DIFFERENT BURIAL TYPES 19
3.4 EXCAVATION 19
3.5 OSL DATING SAMPLES 20
3.6 TEXTURAL ANALYSIS 20
3.7 MICROMORPHOLOGY OF POTTERY 20
3.8 GEOCHEMISTRY 20
3.8.1 Major Oxide 21
3.8.1.1 CIA 21
3.8.2 REE Analysis 21
3.9 FLOTATION 21

Chapter 4 Exploration and Excavation at Siruthavoor 22
4.1 INTRODUCTION 22
4.2 EXPLORATION OF IA-EH BURIAL SITES AROUND SIRUTHAVOOR 22
4.3 SPATIAL PATTERN OF BURIALS AT SIRUTHAVOOR 25
4.3.1 Cairn Circle 38
4.3.2 Dolmen 39
4.3.3 Dolmenoid Cist 41
4.3.4 Cist 41
4.3.5 Urn Burials 42
4.4 LITHOSECTION 43

4.5 EXCAVATION	45
4.5.1 Excavation of Burial 1 (Cairn Circle)	47
4.5.2 Excavation of Burial 2 (Sarcophagus)	49
4.5.4 Excavation of Burial 4 (Dolmen)	53
4.5.5 Excavation of Burial 5 (Dolmen with circle)	54
4.5.6 Excavation of Burial 6 (Dolmenoid Cist)	58
4.5.7 Excavation of Burial 7 (Urn with Capstone)	59
4.5.8 Excavation of Burial 8 (Urn)	60

Chapter 5 Results 61

5.1 LABORATORY ANALYSIS OF SEDIMENTS AND POTTERY FROM SIRUTHAVOOR	61
5.2 TEXTURAL ANALYSIS	61
5.2.1 Trilinear Diagram of Sand, Silt and Clay Percentages	61
5.2.2 Sieve Analyses	61
5.3 GEOCHEMICAL ANALYSIS OF SEDIMENT SAMPLES FROM SIRUTHAVOOR	64
5.3.1 Major Element Analysis of Sediment Samples from Siruthavoor	64
5.3.2 Trace metal data of sediment samples from Siruthavoor	67
5.4 OSL DATING OF POTTERY SAMPLES FROM EXCAVATED BURIALS	68
5.5 ANALYSIS OF POTTERY AT SIRUTHAVOOR	68
5.5.1 REE Data	70
5.5.2 Preliminary Examination of Potsherd Thin Sections from Siruthavoor Megalithic Burial Site	72
5.5.3 Megascopic Observations	73
5.5.4 Microscopic Studies	73
5.5.4.1 Rock fragment and sand temper	73
5.5.4.2 Iron oxide mineralogy in the clays	73
5.5.5 Description of the thin Section	74
5.5.6 Discussion of pottery thin section	76

Chapter 6 Discussion and Conclusion 77

6.1 INTRODUCTION	77
6.2 CHRONOLOGY	77
6.3 EXCAVATION AND EXPLORATION	78
6.3.1 Spatial Analysis of IA-EH Burials	80
6.3.2 Spatial Analysis of IA-EH Burials at Siruthavoor	81
6.3.3 Analysis of Data from Excavation at Siruthavoor	83
6.4 SEDIMENT ANALYSIS OF BURIALS AND LITHOSECTION AT SIRUTHAVOOR	84
6.4.1 Textural Analysis of Burials and Lithosection at Siruthavoor	84
6.4.2 GEOCHEMICAL ANALYSIS OF BURIAL AND LITHOSECTION 1 SEDIMENTS	85
6.5 CONCLUSIONS	86

References 87

List of Figures

Figure 1.1 Map showing excavated sites in Tamil Nadu (map prepared by Kelly G and Haricharan S. 2010) 7
Figure 2.1 The study area: Siruthavoor 14
Figure 2.2 Study area showing 1. encroachment, 2. dolmen with circle and 3. Siruthavoor Lake 15
Figure 2.3 Exposed Statigraphic sections at Siruthavoor 15
Figure 2.4 Large areas of the site destroyed due to natural and anthropogenic activities 17
Figure 3.1 Flow chart showing the different methodologies adopted for understanding the formation of the site 18
Figure 4.1 Study area Siruthavoor and other IA-EH sites around Siruthavoor 22
Figure 4.2 Site Sirukunram: Cairn Circle 23
Figure 4.3 Dolmen with curved cairn circle stones at Siruthavoor 23
Figure 4.4 Dolmen with curved cairn circle stones at Amur 24
Figure 4.5 Dolmen very low in Siruthavoor with 2 large slabs as capstone 24
Figure 4.6 Dolmen very low in Amur with 2 large slabs as capstone 25
Figure 4.7 Dolmen at Amur with anti-chamber and large flat boulder as capstone 25
Figure 4.8 Dolmen at Siruthavoor with anti-chamber and large flat boulder as capstone 26
Figure 4.9 Gnranatic Gneiss and Charnokite used for IA-EH burials at Siruthavoor 26
Figure 4.10 Capstone at Amur showing signs of being shaped 26
Figure 4.11 Capstone from Siruthavoor with a line of holes probably for cutting or shaping of stone 26
Figure 4.12 Map of Siruthavoor showing all the burial types including cairn circle, dolmen, cist, dolmen with circle, cist with circle and dolmenoid cist 27
Figure 4.13 Over all map of Siruthavoor (close up) showing the spatial outlay of all IA-EH burials at Siruthavoor 28
Figure 4.14 Spatial outlay cist and cist with circle type burial at Siruthavoor 29
Figure 4.15 Spatial outlay of dolmen and dolmen with circle type burials at Siruthavoor 30
Figure 4.16 Spatial outlay of cist with circle and dolmen with circle type burials at Siruthavoor 31
Figure 4.17 Spatial outlay of dolmen, cist and dolmenoid cist type of burials at Siruthavoor 32
Figure 4.18 Spatial outlay of cairn circle type burials at Siruthavoor 33
Figure 4.19 Spatial outlay of cist type burials at Siruthavoor 34
Figure 4.20 Spatial outlay cist with circle type burials at Siruthavoor 35
Figure 4.21 Spatial outlay of dolmen with circle type burials at Siruthavoor 36
Figure 4.22 Spatial outlay of dolmen type burial at Siruthavoor 37
Figure 4.23 cairn circle with lateritic blocks outside circle 38
Figure 4.24 Cairn circle around hillock showing overlap of burials 38
Figure 4.25 Dolmen with low/flush capstone 39
Figure 4.26 Dolmen with circle, dolmen has five stones supporting the capstone and is circular shaped 39
Figure 4.27 Low dolmen with long slabs as capstone 39
Figure 4.28 Dolmen with long boulder shaped stones 40
Figure 4.29 Dolmen with outcrop, and open on two sides 40
Figure 4.30 Dolmen with symbolic features and outcrop used as part of a dolmen 40
Figure 4.31 Dolmenoid cist showing swastika pattern and roughly shaped stones 41
Figure 4.32 Dolmenoid cist with swastika pattern at Amur 41
Figure 4.33 Cist burial situated northwest of Siruthavoor Lake with swastika pattern clearly visible on the surface 42
Figure 4.34 Cist burial with one orthostat higher above ground than rest 42
Figure 4.35 Exposed section showing cist burial 42
Figure 4.36 exposed section of cist burial with sarcophagus and urn seen 43
Figure 4.37 Iron implements found near disturbed cist burials during exploration 43
Figure 4.38 Map showing distribution of lithosection at Sairuthavoor 44
Figure 4.39 Graph of lithosections 1-5 45
Figure 4.40 Image showing lithosections 1-5 at Siruthavoor 45
Figure 4.41 Distribution of excavated burials and lithosection at Siruthavoor 46
Figure 4.42 Plan of Burial 1 at Siruthavoor, situated close to the lake, having an extra stone inside the cairn circle in the east ... 47
Figure 4.43 Statigraphy of burial 1 eastern section 48
Figure 4.44 Southwestern quadrant with coarse Red Ware pottery 48
Figure 4.45 Western quadrant showing sarcophagus 49
Figure 4.46 Burial 1 after excavation of eastern and western quadrants showing stone assemblage in the centre 49
Figure 4.47 Burial 2:Exposed sarcophagus with remnants of lid 50
Figure 4.48 Iron implements and beads from excavated burials at Siruthavoor 51
Figure 4.49 Burial 3: Cist type burial with fourth orthostat disturbed 51
Figure 4.50 Outside cist, cairn packing on eastern and south eastern areas 52
Figure 4.51 Slab on top of cist with cairn packing on top with slab in eastern side 52
Figure 4.52 Cist with pottery 53
Figure 4.53 Iron implements from burial 3, sword like object and 2 large iron slabs found near sarcophagus inside cist 53
Figure 4.54 Sarcophagus, large iron implements and Red Ware stand 54
Figure 4.56 Sarcophagus of cist with stone below legs to balance the structure 54
Figure 4.57 sarcophagus from cist with associated grave goods 55
Figure 4.58 Burial 4: dolmen associated with outcrop, next to smaller hillock 55
Figure 4.59 Burial 4 showing association with outcrop 56

Figure 4.60 Burial 5: Dolmen in pentagon/circular shape with two triangular stones in the east 56
Figure 4.61 Burial 5 with stone packing between boulders below captsone 57
Figure 4.62 Gold ring from burial 5 57
Figure 4.63 Sarcophagi A, B and C within burial 5 with remains of lid on top 58
Figure 4.64 Bedrocks on which sarcophagi were kept in burial 5 59
Figure 4.65 Dolmenoid cist type burial, burial 6 59
Figure 4.68 Burial 7, urn with capstone 60
Figure 4.69 Urn with inverted lid on top burial 8 60
Figure 5.1 Trilinear diagram of sediments from burial 1 62
Figure 5.2 Trilinear diagram of sediments from burial 2 62
Figure 5.3 Trilinear diagram of sediments from burial 3 62
Figure 5.4 Trilinear diagram of sediments from burial's 4,5,7 and 8 63
Figure 5.5 Trilinear diagram of sediments from lithosection 1 63
Figure 5.6 The figure represents depth (cm) versus ratios Al2O3 /FeO, Si/Al and LOI, CIA, SiO2, Al2O3 indicating geochemical break between 70-80 cm 67
Figure 5.7 Ni versus Cr values of burial sediments and lithosection 1 indicate local source and post Archaean origin 69
Figure 5.8 Red Ware stand from Burial 3 with graffiti mark at the base 70
Figure 5.9 Black and Red Ware cup from burial 7 70
Figure 5.10 Pottery from Burial 3 showing graffiti marks 70
Figure 5.11 REE data normalized using PASS values of clay samples from Siruthavoor and a potter from Chennai 71
Figure 5.12 REE data normalized using PASS values of pottery samples from burials 1, 5, 7 and 8 72
Figure 5.13 Shapes of Various pottery pieces from Siruthavoor excavation 72
Figure 5.14 (a-d) Photomicrographs of the potsherd thin sections 74
Figure 5.14 (e-j) Photomicrographs of the potsherd thin sections 75
Figure 5.14 (k-l) Photomicrographs of the potsherd thin sections 76
Figure 6.1 Plan of IA-EH burials at Ramalai, in Upper Palar region (after Darshana 1997) 80
Figure 6.2 Plan of IA-EH burials at Kargur, in Upper Palar region (after Darshana 1997) 80
Figure 6.3 Plan of IA-EH burials at Pogalur, in Upper Palar region (after Darshana 1997) 80
Figure 6.4 Plan of IA-EH burials at Poongulam, in Upper Palar region (after Darshana 1997) 80
Figure 6.5 Plan of IA-EH burials of Kodumanal (after Rajan 1997) 81
Figure 6.6 Plan of Brahmagiri, with Area A,B and C marked and spatially separated from each other (after Wheeler 1948) 81
Figure 6.7 Plan of Area's B and C of Brahmagiri (after Wheeler 1948) 82
Figure 6.8 Different types of dolmen from Siruthavoor, using long dressed and undressed slabs 82
Figure 6.9 Different cairn circle burials at Siruthavoor located in different areas of the site 85

List of Tables

Table 1.1 Correlation between sites and type of burial of coastal sites in Tamil Nadu 9
Table 1.2 Correlation between site and artifact excavated of coastal sites in Tamil Nadu 10
Table 1.3 Correlations between sites and type of burial of inland sites in Tamil Nadu 11
Table 1.4 Dates from Previously Excavated IA-EH Sites 11
Table 1.5 Classification of burials put forward by several archaeologists 12
Table 2.1 Stratigraphy of the Siruthavoor site 16
Table 2.2 Major plant varieties found around Chennai 16
Table 2.3 Some varieties of Acacia found growing around Chennai 17
Table 4.1. Individual type of burial and their number 25
Table 5.1 Textural analysis of burial 1 61
Table 5.2 Textural Analysis of Burial 2 61
Table 5.3 Textural Analysis of Burial 3 61
Table 5.4 Textural analysis of burials 4, 5, 7 and 8 61
Table 5.5 Textural analysis of lithosection 1 61
Table 5.6 Statistically analyzed sieving data of Burial 1 63
Table 5.7 Statistically analyzed sieving data of Burial 2 64
Table 5.8 Statistically analyzed sieving data of Burial 3 64
Table 5.9 Statistically analyzed sieving data of Burial's 4, 5,7 and 8 64
Table 5.10 Statistically analyzed sieving data of Lithosection 1 1 65
Table 5.11 Major elemental data of burial 1 65
Table 5.12 Major elemental data of Burial 2 65
Table 5.13 Major elemental data of Burial 3 65
Table 5.14 Major elemental data of burial 4,5, 7 and 8 66
Table 5.15 Major elemental data of lithosection 1 66
Table 5.16 Major elemental and CIA data of burial 1 66
Table 5.17 Major elemental and CIA data of burial 2 66
Table 5.18 Major elemental and CIA data of burial 3 66
Table 5.19 Major elemental and CIA data of burial 4, 5, 7 and 8 66
Table 5.20 Major elemental and CIA data of lithosection 1 67
Table 5.21 Trace metal data of sediment samples of burial 1 68
Table 5.22 Trace metal data of sediment samples of burial 2 68
Table 5.23 Trace metal data of sediment samples of burial 3 68
Table 5.24 Trace metal data of sediment samples of burial 4, 5, 7 and 8 68
Table 5.25 Trace metal data of sediment samples of lithosection 1 68
Table 5.26 OSL dates of pottery 68
Table 5.27 REE data normalized using PAAS values of clay samples from Siruthavoor and a present day potter from Chennai 71
Table 5.28 REE data normalized using PASS values of pottery samples from burials 1, 5, 7 and 8 71
Table 6.1 Dates from excavated burial pottery 78

Acknowledgment

I had been studying and working in archaeology since 2002, but learning and talking about Geology, in the Department of Geology, Anna University as a Ph.D student did not come easily. Dr. S. Srinivasalu was very patient and I am very grateful for all the support and knowledge I received. I would like to thank Dr. L. Elango for the encouragement he has extended towards all my endeavors. I would also like to thank Dr. S. Sanjeevi, who was the Head of the Department when I first applied for a PhD program in Anna University. Vinod R.V. and Thomas Babu gave me their unconditional help with field work and mapping. They have both helped me with the field survey, and have been largely responsible for the maps of the sites in this research. I am also thankful to Aravind, Vasu P., Sreekanth K.S., Swathi G., Krishnaraj, Ganesh, Satish C., Vikram N., Divya V., Nagasunder, Babu, Ramesh, Prasana, and Anand K. for all their help with the field work. Each one of them accompanied me to the site and helped me with the field survey, sometimes more than once. I would like to thank Prasad G., Navin S., Arun K., and Veena MP for their support and constant guidance. I would like to thank ICHR for the fellowship I received from them. I thank Sathyabhama Badreenath, the Superintending of Archaeology, Chennai Circle, the ASI (Chennai Circle) and the Archaeological Survey of India, New Delhi, for granting us permission to carry out the excavation. While from the moment I saw Siruthavoor I knew I wanted to map the burials there, the excavation of this site was an unexpected but lucky break, for which I have to thank both my PhD supervisor Prof. Hema Achyuthan and Ms. Sathyabhama Badhreentath and the ASI. During the excavation Mr. K.P.Mohandas, Mr. V.Sarangadharan and Mr.G.Margabandu who were the resource people from ASI, Chennai circle were very supportive. I am grateful to Selvakumar V, Darshana S, Jayshree P and Jinu K for the many drafts they have read of these chapters and helped me keep the important sections and weed out the parts which were not necessary. I would also like to thank Dr. Gwendolyn Kelly for all her help with the pottery drawings. I would like to specially thank Prof. Hema Achyuthan, least of all for the innumerable trips to the canteen for chai and a chat-invariably about Siruthavoor, for all her patience and forbearance and for all the times she fought on my behalf. I would like to thank my family, who have without hesitation supported me through all my trials and tribulations, and every real and imagined crisis this research has thrown my way. I would especially like to thank my sisters for always being there for me. I would like to thank Professor Robin Dennell for encouraging me to submit this manuscript for publication. I would also like to convey my heartfelt thanks to the publishers, especially Dr. David Davison. I also thank all my friends, Dhanush, Ramji, Setji, David and all the people of Siruthavoor who have helped in small but invaluable ways without expecting anything in return.

SMRITI HARICHARAN

Preface

This publication is a result of the work I had carried out during my PhD thesis. I have used the spelling Siruthavoor both here and in my PhD thesis submitted in May 2010, while the ASI used Siruthavur and the village census (http://www.census2011.co.in) refers to it as Sirudavoor. It seems that the village is referred to by all three spellings in various sources. The reason I choose to work here for my thesis was because there were so many different types of burials located in this site, and even in 2006 sand quarrying had left its scars on the IA-EH landscape. Many of the burials were exposed on a daily basis, and completely destroyed in a few days. There has been lot of previous published research on the megalithic burials especially in the Chengapattu-an administrative sub division of north Tamilnadu. And yet I felt it was astonishing that there were hardly any maps of these Iron Age-Early Historical burial sites either for this region or even much of south India.

In 2006 a colleague mentioned the existence of an amazing 'megalithic' site near Chennai and one afternoon I decided to visit the site. I must have seen only 1/4th of the site on that visit but was entranced by the different burial types. I could also see semi intact burials and their associated pottery within the sections exposed from sand quarrying, which had just begun to take place at Siruthavoor. I started my Ph.D subsequently and in 2007 had begun to survey and map the burials at Siruthavoor. Around this time my PhD supervisor Prof. Hema Achyuthan decided to apply for a permit to excavate the site along with Ms. Sathyabhama Badhreenath, who was at that time the Superintending Archaeologist, for the Chennai Circle of ASI. The ASI provided the funding for the excavation and the resource persons for drawing and archaeologists for supervision, while Anna University provided technical assistance, funding for post field work analysis such as the OSL dating and myself as a research Assistant to work at the excavation.

We excavated the site over a period of three months with a gap of a few weeks in between. My own duties included supervision as well as recording field notes. I am grateful that the ASI team were supportive of the fact that this would be a part of my PhD thesis and allowed me to take part in the decision making and direction of the excavation. I was indeed very lucky to not only take part in the excavation but also be trained in some aspects of directing an excavation. After the completion of the excavation I had shared all my field notes and photographs with them, while they shared their photographs. Most of my own chapter on excavation as well as their monograph (Badhreenath 2011) are based on these field notes.

Since 2006 I have visited Siruthavoor multiple times and have slowly watched the site being completely altered due to sand quarrying. During one such visit, I remember watching an inhabitant of the village measuring some land to sell, within which there was a dolmen. Foreseeing that this was indeed a death warrant for this burial, and in an attempt to convey its significance, I said 'do you know this is a burial and your ancestor maybe buried here?' to which the reply was 'how old is it?' and I said 'probably some 2000 years' pat came the reply 'oh in that case how is it connected to me?'. As Dixon (1982) states our (academic) temptation is to treat these works according to the model of our own symbolic activity and of what we think we know about the symbolic activity of our immediate predecessors. And yet at Siruthavoor I knew people were curious about what I was doing (literally in their backyards at times) but did not identify with it, they were in some ways awed by the age and the concept of people of the past and their achievements, but did not feel that this meant it had to be preserved.

In 2010, I had worked for four years, the villagers knew me, and I knew some of them. Sometimes during my visits if I was alone, and surveying within the reserve forest which was north of the village, and into which the site expanded, some of the younger boys from the village would come with me since they believed the forest was not safe. During the excavations many of them visited the site, and I spoke to them about what we were finding. Once a group of women form the village were chatting with me about the excavation and they were talking about how if we had found teeth we could have figured out the dietary habits of the IA-EH people.

And yet after the excavation whenever I visited, they would ask me half in jest if I was going to have them evicted from their land. The logic for them was that I had brought a government body (the ASI) to work in their village, which had in turn brought media attention (journalists who reported the excavation). They knew that this land within the archaeological site was located was contested, and yet the village politicians had promised them portions of this land. The sand or stone quarrying they carried out earned them very little, it was the more well off villagers who made the money. Many spoke to me about lack of medical facilities, hard working conditions and minimal income within the already limited options.

They were interested in the excavation and curious about my work, but understandably, did not see the need to put the preservation of these burials above their own daily struggles. Eventually most of the site was partitioned into parcels of land, divided between the villagers and sold to people from Chennai. These people from the city, cleared the burials, built fences and grew banana trees within their plots. They did not plan to live there, as far as I could tell it was an investment. This is not a unique story in any way, but it does underline the importance of mapping these sites. It is impractical to believe that we can preserve all the IA-EH burials or habitation sites around Chennai, as the city grows, villages like Siruthavoor will disappear, and soon there will remain no trace here of an archaeological site, but for Siruthavoor there are maps of where the burials once stood!

Chapter 1
Introduction

1.1 WHY STUDY THE MEGALITHS IN SOUTH INDIA

Archeological artifacts such as stone tools, ceramics, coins, metal implements, and ornaments like beads, are generally used to evaluate and understand the history of humans. These artifacts are especially important for the study of periods that lack concrete literary evidence. Intangible aspects such as spiritual beliefs and ceremonies, as well as tangible but perishable objects, are lost in the passage of time but artifacts are more likely to survive the vicissitudes of time. Pollen analysis, plant ecology and not least prehistoric archaeology have contributed to the recognition of the transitional zone between uncontaminated nature and what eventually became known a cultural landscape (Fagri 1988). Cultural landscapes are looked upon not only as products of human intervention, but also and in particular as the result of human desire to leave an imprint of control and power, often associated with territoriality and religious or political ambitions (Sahlqvist 2001). Megalithic burials, which are found in vast numbers in southern and central India, are a well-known global phenomenon and their builders have left behind a landscape altered by their funereal remains.

This study aims at using and understanding man-land relationships in order to better comprehend the megalithic burials of Tamil Nadu. Funereal remains are one of the most important lingering means of understanding society, customs and religion of pre and proto historic periods. Many questions remain unanswered for the Iron Age of south India, and the megalithic burials are an important piece of this puzzle. This site specific study helps us better understand some aspects such as spatial distribution, chronology and post depositional changes of the burials at Siruthavoor.

1.2 USING THE TERM: 'MEGALITHIC'

Originally, the term 'megalithic' was applied to tombs, standing stones, circle stones and isolated standing stones in western and northern Europe. The criteria for the application of this term to artifacts and monuments included not merely the existence of big stones, but also required evidence of function and ritualism (Childe 1945). Tilley (1999) provides interesting analysis on the use of the term megalithic. Previously restricted in usage, it was more frequently used in the 1960s and later, more cautiously, with the advent of the "processual" and "post processual" schools of archaeology.

The debate on the origin of megaliths is ongoing and the attempt to define the megalithic 'culture' has been made since before the 1910's (Childe 1945). Smith (1915) uses the invention of the steam engine as an analogy to argue his point, suggesting that a systematic development/invention like a megalithic burial must have originated in/from a common geographic location. Lewis (1916), on the other hand, suggests that the origin of megalithic monuments was not from one center, but that the vast number and distance between countries in which they developed implies a local or tribal, rather than a singular custom. Smith (1915) further comments that while the idea of a steam engine had been thought of by many people/in many places it was brought to perfection only in one place/ by one person. While this is an interesting analogy, unlike the steam engine, it is difficult to define a perfect megalith. Each type of megalith is modeled by a distinct culture to meet the ritualistic or functional needs of a specific social group. The arrival of scientific dating techniques such as 14 C altered the way we think of these theories (Pollard 2013).

While the idea of megalithic burials may or may not have originated from one central point, in India these burials exhibit regional variations that do not always appear to be based merely on the available resources. The ritual behavior that takes place as a part of death rites of passage has been described to vary over a spatial and temporal context (Chapman 1995). The study of megalithic burials around the world has resulted in varied theories dealing with different geological and geographic motivations for the location of the megalithic sites: geotectonic settings; seismic zoning; sunshine activity; climatic peculiarities; areas of thunderbolts and hailstones; local background radioactivity (related to the rocks); and geomorphologic (landscape) location and orientation (Kostov 2008). However, while exploring various theories on territorial behavior using funerary remains on a landscape, Chapman (1995) states that the megaliths needs to be understood within a regional context and not just a localized pattern. Much like a microscope, wherein different magnifications can show you different aspects of a sample, constant readjustment of the scale, is important to the understanding of a concept as widespread and varying as the megaliths of south India.

Cooney (2000) draws attention to the question of why these monumental traditions emerged, and, in the context of the Irish megalithic, he states that often the landscape has been preceded and succeeded by other cultures. One reason why the megalithic burials draw our attention is because of their visibility in the landscape, which Cooney (2000) concludes implies that the people raising the monuments not only thought of the past but also the future. The use of megalithic burials to understand the social context/ divisions, marking/territorial behavior on the landscape has been previously debated, using case studies as well as ethnography (Chapman 1995, Tilley 2004, Hodder 1992, Kostov 2008). The term "megalithic" is a word all archaeologists know, though not a common everyday term like cave art and, inspite of various new theories and discoveries that have occurred, the term remains durably in usage (Tilley 1999). The shortcomings with the usage of the term 'megalithic' in terms of the south Indian context has been discussed previously (Moorti 1994, Mohanty and Selvakumar 2002, Morrison et al 2008, Haricharan et al 2013, Haricharan and Keerthi 2014). However we continue to use this term, this maybe as Tilley (1999) suggests a testament to the durability of the term, yet it is important to remind ourselves of its limitations and keep an open mind towards possible alternatives. The terms Iron Age-Early Historic (hence forth IA-EH) will be used instead of megalithic in context to the burials within the larger study area of this book i.e. northern Tamilnadu in this paper. However the term megalithic is retained while referring to the larger Indian context since they are chronologically varied and using the term IA-EH for all 'megalithic' burials even within south India would be problematic.

1.3 CHRONOLOGY AND DISTRIBUTION OF MEGALITHIC BURIALS AROUND THE WORLD

The European megaliths have been studied often in terms of landscape and their geometric construction, even coining the term the megalithic yard, provenance etc. (Cowan 1970, Thom and Thom 1978, Thom 1978, Tilley 1999, Cooney 2000). The European megaliths are dated to the fourth millennium BCE and extend till the first millennium BCE (Thom 1978). On an island called Menorca, Spain, megalithic burials including dolmens have been built since the second millennium BCE. Similar to the Indian megaliths they are of different types, having similar grave goods, such as pottery, iron implements and disarticulated skeletal remains, and are spread over the islands of Mallorca and Menorca (Gili et al 2006). The details of the Indian and the Menorca burials are definitely different. While the Menorca burials building practice comes to an end around 800 BCE, the Indian megaliths continue till around 600 CE (Gili et al 2006). The former also had thousands of complete or fragmentary human bones buried in each complex, and dating implies that some graves could have been used for over 300 years (Gili et al 2006). The Indian megaliths, on the other hand, have similar traces of reuse, but the quantity of individual skeletal remains is restricted to less than 10 in each grave (Moorti 1994).

Most scholars date the megalithic monuments of Bulgaria to the Iron Age (1200-500 BCE) on the basis of excavated finds, but there is a suspicion that some of the sites may well date to an earlier period, perhaps even to the Chalcolithic (5000-3500 BCE) (Kostov 2008). Some work has been done to compile the occurrence of various forms of megalithic burials, like the dolmen, around the world (Mackie 1977, Michell 1982, Joussaume 1988). Sjogren (2009) talks about the Swedish megaliths, and the earliest references to these structures referencing them as being built by giants. In fact he states that before the adoption of the Three Age System, one of the terms used in Sweden was the 'Cairn Age' and some authors believed this to be the age of giants, to which period the megaliths belonged. As Midgley (2009) says with reference to the European megaliths in particular, 'modern megalithic scholarship has come a long way from the earliest concerns with these structures, but we have lost none of the fascination that originally inspired the early students of these monuments'.

Megalithic monuments and burials have also been found throughout Africa, the direction of the research with regards to these sites varies from astrological to funeral in nature (Wendorf and Schild 1998, Rao and Libeska 2005, Lawson 2001, Rao 2007). Some of the studies conducted include surveys and excavations in the western African region of Senegal and Gambia (Lawson 2001). The megalithic burials around the Senegambian region is connected to the Axum Empire which dates to around the first century CE, and evidences indicate trade with many ancient empires including India (Butzer 1981). Previous data reveal that these societies had distinct burial and ritual practices that can be seen in the excavated sites of Mai-temenenay (400 BCE) and tomb site of Emba-Derho (400 A.D.) (Rao and Libeska 2005). There is some amount of debate on the dating of megaliths in the Senegambian region (Hill 1978). Boivin et al (2009) mention the existence in Oman of Hafit-type cairn circles of the late fourth millennium BCE while discussing trade contacts between India and Arabia. Cairn-burial sites have been reported and extend from Zhob-Loralai in Pakistani Baluchistan to Kirman and Fars in Iran. The internal evidence from the cairns includes Parthian coins of 1st century BCE, and a Sassanian coin of the 7th century A.D. (Chakrabarti 1977).

Recent exploration and mapping of sites situated on the Madaba Plain in the highlands of central Jordan describe dolmens around al-Murayghat (Savage and Dubis 2002). The excavators report that very few associated pottery and no skeletal remains have been found. Most of the dolmens had clean stone floors; open on one side, with and without stone circles. Dating of the megalithic burials here is unclear due to lack of material; however the fortification walls have been said to belong to the early Bronze age, dating from c. 3500-2000 BCE (Savage 2001, Savage and Dubis 2002). The Mekong River is said to be the artery of Mainland Southeast Asia through which trade and transport were negotiated, and the delta near the coast is where a large centre with strong influences from Indian culture emerged in the first century CE (Sayavongkhamdy and Bellwood 2000, Kallen 2000).

Jar burials are increasingly being found on the Southeast Asian mainland, in Vietnam, Laos (Lao Pako) and Thailand, as well as in northern Sri Lanka. The eastern extremity of jar burial distribution is represented by Yayoi period graves (3rd BCE – 2nd CE) on the island of Kyushu (Gupta 2005).

The finding of pottery very similar in style to that found at Arikamedu, as well as the jar burials, have added to the theory of their common origin (Gupta 2005). Closer to southern India are the megaliths from Sri Lanka, wherein recent pollen analysis and dating of the burials have been carried out (Premathilake, and Seneviratne 2015). The comparisons drawn between megalithic burials of India with the European and non European megaliths have been explored in the past (Smith 1915, Childe 1945, Leshnik 1974, Allchin and Allchin 1982). Asthana (1976) explores the similarity between megaliths of Arabia and those of India, specifically drawing parallels between the Palestine and Kerala graves. While the existence of burials in various parts of the world and their integral similarity has been well documented, their common origin is no longer given much thought. Megalithic burials are found in varying shapes, sizes and forms, over many chronological sequences, and understand their individual characteristics in context with their immediate landscape is important.

1.4 THE IRON AGE-EARLY HISTORIC OR 'MEGALITHIC' BURIALS OF INDIA

With respect to the Indian megalithic burials, it is known that the burials are regionally spread over the Vindhyas, Deccan and peninsular India (Moorti 1994). The origin and distribution of the megalithic burials has often been debated (Smith 1915, Hunt 1924, Childe 1945, Gururaja Rao 1972, Leshnik 1974, Narasimhaiah 1980, Allchin and Allchin 1982, Reddy 1991, Misra 2001, Mohanty and Selvakumar 2002). Leshnik (1974) states that three questions that can help us understand the problems of these burials are: who made them, at what time and in what cultural-historical context? If we are to accept these three as the questions that will help us understand megaliths better, we are yet to answer any of them completely.

Megalithic burials in India are mainly found across the five states of Maharashtra, Tamil Nadu, Karnataka, Kerala and Andhra Pradesh, although some scattered burials are also seen in the north and northeastern areas of India (Moorti 1994, Mohanty and Selvakumar 2002). Moorti (1994) illustrates the number of megalithic sites in India are as follows, Maharashtra has 43 burial (only) sites, while Andhra Pradesh has 168, Karnataka 429, Tamil Nadu 423, and Kerala 196. Interestingly, his data indicates that memorial stones in Tamil Nadu (68) and Kerala (73) are far more in number than Karnataka and Andhra Pradesh (25). However, in the last 10 decades more explorations, surveys and excavation has been carried out; Rajan et al (2009) reports more than 2,500 sites in Tamil Nadu and 866 sites in Kerala. Large cemetery sites include as many as 1,500 graves, although a majority of the nearly 2,000 reported sites in south India consists of less than 10 graves (Sinopoli 2002). There is evidence of uneven distribution of sites within Tamil Nadu, Kerala, Karnataka and Andhra Pradesh and little systematic survey has been carried out to define the density and scope of the sites (Sinopoli 2002). Studies on the megaliths in India have focused on creating and understanding a typological classification, contextualizing the literary evidence found of this period and excavating burials (Srinivasan 1946, Krishnaswami and Saran 1955-1956, 1956-1957, 1957-1958, Banerjee and Soundararajan 1959, Thapar 1971, Gururaja Rao 1972, Narasimhaiah 1980, Moorti 1994, Rajan 2000, Misra 2001, Mohanty and Selvakumar. 2002). There is a desperate need to uncover further data from these sites through topographical mapping and recovery of artifacts.

Evidence from the human skeletal record of prehistoric India suggests that diet supplementation and gene flow between settled and mobile traders has existed for at least four millennia. This implies considerable antiquity for the close relationships between hunter-gatherers and urban agriculturalists (Lukacs 1990). In the above study, Lukacs (1990) largely used skeletal records from Harappan and others sites from the north of India, yet these studies strengthen already existing ideas of the hazy line existing between social groups in the Indian context. Chattopadhyaya (1996) has studied the ethnographic and archaeological evidence that supports the Saxe-Goldstein formulation on the interrelationship between cemeteries and corporate group rights to crucial resources. He further states that amongst the lineage based group, the Mundas of the Chhota Nagpur hills of southern Bihar, land is precious and inherited within the family. Each clan has its own *Sasan*, or formal disposal area for the dead, situated on one side of the village. This supports the idea that it is possible that, within a site, certain families/clans had inherited rights over certain spatial areas thereby giving another possible explanation to different types of burials within a single megalithic site.

The megalithic burials are influenced by the local geology and rock types to some extent; for example, in Maharashtra a large number of stone circles are found, while rock cut chambers and topikal are seen in Kerala and Menhirs in Andhra Pradesh, Karnataka and Kerala (Reddy 1991, Babington 1823). Two important aspects of the megalithic burial are the availability of raw material, i.e., the geological features, and the social aspect of the burials, i.e., the ceremonial and emotional characteristics of the burial. Two possible motivations for any aspect related to culture and society's reaction to death are firstly, to preserve the body along with relics of the person, and secondly, to put the dead out of sight. Ethnographic and archaeological evidences indicate that in India burial preceded cremation (Crooke 1899).

In case social differences did emerge during the Iron Age, literary and archaeological evidence are the best clues available. Settlement during the Iron Age appears to have been spatially diverse. They vary in size, and some with specialized economic production occur in a wider variety of settings than during the Neolithic period (Bauer et al 2007). Gallon (2008) has also analysed iron objects from excavated sites in Karnataka, Maski, Brahmagiri, and Kadebakele in the context of habitation and IA-EH sites, and the megalithic burials seem to have a higher percentage of tools and weapons. He concludes that construction materials are positively associated with habitation areas, weapons are negatively associated with habitation areas, and tools appear in both contexts at expected frequencies. Brubaker (2001) states on the assumption that the megaliths were restricted to higher status individuals, weapons probably served as symbols of social inequalities and as mechanisms for physically maintaining such differences. The high visibility of these objects and their similar forms across the study sites may indicate that they also carried messages regarding inter-group affiliations. Objects such as beads and bangles are made of metal, most often copper, bronze or gold. Conversely, metal objects that are not ornamental are almost exclusively made of iron, suggesting distinctions between the social value of iron and other metals (Gallon 2008).

1.5 THE SANGAM LITERATURE AND IA-EH BURIALS OF TAMILNADU

Sangam literature has been used often to understand social aspects of the period contemporary with the IA-EH burials of Tamil Nadu. Contextualising the archaeological and historical data together would contribute much towards an understanding of the Iron Age (Abraham 2003). While few scholars still question it, most scholars date the composition of the *Sangam* poems, if not their compilation into anthologies, to the 3rd BCE -3rd CE (Pillai 1986, Nilakantasastri 1966, Sivathamby 1974, Stein 1977, Subrahmanian 1986, Narayanan 1988, Zvelebil 1992, Gurukkal 1993, Champakalakshmi 1996, Heitzman 1997, Hart 2004). Besides the *Sangam* anthology, other sources of evidence such as stone edicts, copper plates from Tamil Nadu, the Asokan inscriptions, as well as foreigners' accounts, help corroborate to some extent the dating of the anthology (Subrahmanian 1986, Zvelebil 1992, Heitzman 1997, Abraham 2003).

The *Sangam* literature has been open to possible alteration, manipulation or even forgery due to political and religious motives in later periods. It is also known that the palm leaf manuscripts were not always well preserved or copied and a lot of data has been lost (Zvelebil 1992, Heitzman 1997). The usefulness of the literary evidence in the study of the socio-economic nature of ancient Tamil Nadu has been debated upon by many scholars (Sivathamby 1974, Srinivasa Iyengar 1983). However one thing that is strongly brought forward through these debates is that there is a danger in the literal interpretation of the *Sangam* poems. Trinkaus (1984) highlights the pitfalls of complete reliance on literary evidence, which is subject to manipulation to meet the needs of the society contemporary with the literature in question. He states that reliance on written documents alone requires communication between individuals separated in space and/or time, which is not possible. With respect to the archaeological data, many of the excavation reports are subject to the excavator's unique descriptive methods. This then results in the fact that some details which may be considered important in an geoarchaeological context or certain specific details about the Iron age-Early Historic burials and habitation sites are not available for study. The choices of which burials are excavated have also been made to fulfill the aims of each particular excavation, making a comparison between the individual sites harder.

Another factor is that each site may contain a roughly estimated average of over a 100 burials; however, the number of burials excavated is generally less than 10. For e.g., at Tiruvakkarai, South Arcot district, only four out of an estimated total of over 100 burials were excavated (IAR 84-85). Out of the four burials dug in the second season of excavation at Kunnattur, Chengalputtu district, and one burial had no skeletal remains and limited grave goods (IAR 56-57). However, this was a result of the burial chosen and does not necessarily reflect on all the burials at that site. This implies that the data we have is roughly 4% of the complete data, which then means that the information we have is unintentionally biased. Considering how unique and variable the IA-EH burials even within a particular site are, this leaves us blind to a lot of information. Nevertheless, an attempt has been made to try to compare and understand the excavated material using a tabular column (Tables 1.1 to 1.3).

1.6 SOCIAL AND ECONOMIC STRUCTURE OF THE IRON AGE-EARLY HISTORICAL PERIOD BASED ON LITERARY SOURCES AND THE ARCHAEOLOGICAL EVIDENCE

Tamil literature talks about the five different divisions based on their physiographic location, each following its own individual customs and mode of living. These five landscapes are *marutam, kurunji, mullai, neithal, palai* (Sesha Iyengar 1982, Srinivasa Iyengar 1983, Gurukkal 1993, Rajayyan 2005). Of interest to the study of the IA-EH burials, these divisions were not just with reference to their geographic location but also their separate systems of social, economic and political structure. The people of *marutam* landscape were the agriculturists, the people of *kurunji* zone were semi agriculturists, the people of the *mullai* region were pastoral, people of *neithal* zone were fishermen and the inhabitants of the *palai* landscape the hunters (Sivathamby 1974, Sesha Iyengar 1982). Within the eastern coast of Tamil Nadu, besides the fishermen, other culturally or socially different communities cohabited. The literary evidence points to a complex system of kinship, clan and various modes of habitation such as *Kudi, cheri* and *nadu*. For more on the *tinai* system from the *Sangam* literature and the archaeological data from the IA-EH sites of north Tamilnadu see Haricharan and Keerthi (2014).

It has also been hypothesized that agriculture (*marutam*) may have taken a while longer to develop and a strong pastoral, subsistence agricultural system may have co-existed along with a hunter gatherer system (Raman 1974, Seneviratne 1995). The *tinai* system is important for an understanding of the socio-economic development in the Tamil country (Champakalakshmi 1996). Rajan (2000) draws attention to the fact that a large number of references are made to urn burials in the *Sangam* literature and his explanation for it is that the majority of *Sangam* literature is in connection to the *marutam* region. From topographical data we can speculate that the urn burials are found largely in the *marutam* region, which is the fertile delta region, due to lack of availability of stone.

Assuming that this dynamic society mentioned in the literature evolved over a period of time, it seems obvious that it must have had some reference in an earlier period. On the basis of this reasoning, the IA-EH burial system and the evolving social and economic structure would surely have impacted if not stimulated each other. Two factors that added impetus to the urbanization were the trade system and agriculture, and its main impact is seen in the *marutam* and *neihtal* eco-zones (Champakalakshmi 1996). The diversification of agricultural production and the use of both wild and domesticated animals in Iron Age and Early Historic life likely accompanied changing logistics, understandings, and cultural valuations that can be linked to emerging social differences (Bauer et al 2007). Previous research has assumed that towns probably first arose from the bartering of products; the literature refers to the coastal communities that manufactured salt, which was of great demand (Sesha Iyengar 1982).

On the coast of Tamil Nadu, excavations have revealed that amongst others Arikamedu, Korkai, Karaikadu, Alagankulam, Vasavasamudram and Kaveripattinam are port sites, highlighting the existence of trade contacts and outside cultural influences (Begley 1983, Sridhar 2004, Sridhar 2005) (Fig 1.2). Suttukeni which has IA-EH burials can be dated to 2nd century BCE and this suggests an overlap with the early stages of the port site at Arikamedu. It is also known that the two sites are about 20 kilometers apart, so while we may not know what interaction existed between them, some contact seems probable (Begley 1983). We know from the excavations at Arikamedu that the structures seem to be industrial-commercial in nature and the residential area, if it existed at all, remains unexcavated. However Arikamedu is an exception, for unlike other South Indian port sites that have only had sporadic contacts with the west, it had continuous and flourishing trade over a long period of time (Begley 1983). What this illustrates is that while this period had habitation sites on the scale of a cluster of huts, as well as urbanized centers and ports contemporaneously.

The sporadic urbanization correlates well with the habitation variance within the *tinai* system. For instance, the *neithamakkal* have *pattinam/pakkam* (villages) and the agriculturists have *ur/perur* (big village) and the semi agriculturists who lived in the hilly region had habitation which consisted of clusters of *sirukudi* (huts) (Sesha Iyengar 1982). Literary evidence has special relevance here as it helps us understand the complete lack of habitation sites for most IA-EH sites. It seems probable that if there were fewer large habitation sites compared to the smaller sites referred to in the literature as huts, the poor preservation of these remains would make it difficult to find archaeological remains of bricks and walls. Evidence of rice cultivation and domestic cattle from the Iron age and Early Historic period has been gathered from mt DNA analysis and analysis of organic matter, using the structural appearance of grains and husk markings in pottery, however there is limited data both spatially and chronologically (Fuller and Qin 2009, Chen et al 2010). While evidence of cultivation of rice has been excavated in China, the data for agriculture in south India is mainly from analysis of grains recovered from excavation (Fuller and Qin 2009, Fuller 2009).

A study of the Neolithic period of north-west European loess zone shows a marked difference between the Neolithic period of Central and Western Europe. The former has more settlement sites than burials, the later is the inverse. It seems that the burials are the only element of permanence in Western Europe. This implies that while the settlement acted as a means of keeping the community together in one case, the monument and its rituals did the same job in the second case (Sherratt 1990). The IA-EH burials of Tamil Nadu obviously are contextually different; however, it is possible to speculate that some sort of communal spirit is an essential factor for people who are making iron, growing crops and herding animals whether in Europe or in India. *Sangam* literature talks of villages, urban centers and cluster of huts, as well as trade, agriculture, hunting and pastoralism. The juxtaposition of IA-EH burials in this background makes them more complicated to interpret and understand.

According to Rajayyan (2005) the S*angam* literature and foreigner's accounts imply that a vast majority of the people lived a tribal or "primitive" lifestyle and yet sectors of people made considerable progress in their cultural pursuit. Sesha Iyengar (1982) states that the *Sangam* literature gives evidence for the existence of class, caste, cultural and social differences. The economy described by the *Sangam* literature was an ensemble of unevenly developed forms of production pursued by a society of decent groups who interacted with one another (Gurukkal 1993). Economically, what was earlier a kin labor system was transforming into a more feudal system (Vanamamalai 1973). Literary evidence seems to indicate a change in the social structure of this period and the rise of a class system (Vanamamalai 1973, Gurukkal 1993). Even within a social set up, there seems to be a complex relationship between people, family/

communities. Heitzman (1997) stresses more on the system of honorable gift, and services through heroism and munificence, as well as constant raids and campaigns amongst the three main dynasties of the period.

Literary evidence talks of the Kurumbas who lived in the Palar and Pennar region (*tondaimandalam*). They were attacked by *Athondai* (illegitimate son of Karikal Chozha), who then subjugated them, a pastoral community, in order to tame the "barbarous people" of the region (Sesha Iyengar 1982). This suggests the existence of intra regional cultural differences as well as an awareness of these differences. Heitzman (1997) states that agrarian surplus and commercial taxation was in effect but to a lesser extent than in later periods. The probable existence of multiple systems/ levels of economy and social structure, and the lack of a better understanding of these structures, makes it harder to interpret the period. The *tolkappiyam* also talks of some sort of caste division (*anandanar*-priestly community, *arasar*-warrior, *tatchan*-carpenter, *vellalan*-agriculturists, *vaisyas*-merchants, *paradavar*- fishermen, *umanar*-salt merchants, etc.) though the following of each community was by will and not by traditional obligation (Rajayyan 2005). Unlike the class (or even caste) system of present day, it seems more of a division based on occupation and the influence of the hierarchy on social practices is unclear. While this has not been seen in the archaeological data, the rise in violent war-like activities has been reflected in the archaeological remains from IA-EH burials which make up 1/3rd to 2/3rd the percentage of all the iron artifacts ever excavated (Vanamamalai 1973, Deo 1985). According to Leshnik (1974) this also may also be reflective of a largely non-agriculturist and more pastoral society, which may have been mobile.

1.7 ARCHAEOLOGICAL EVIDENCE FROM EXCAVATED SITES

A complex relationship probably existed between the agriculturists, non agriculturists, producers and other participants of the society, a coexistence of hegemony and discordance on which social formation was based (Gurukkal 1993). In certain respects the collection of south Asian skeletal remains is better documented palaeontologically and archaeologically than aspects of the history of man's biological evolution in Eurasia, Africa, Australasia, and the Americas (Kennedy 1975, Kennedy 1980). The IA-EH burials, generally contain post-excarnate fractional human skeletal remains of usually more than one individual (Sundara 1979). Dental pathology studies done at Mahurjhari showed that the people occupying the area were agriculturally oriented, with a diet of soft carbonate food (Lukacs 1981). Skeletal remains from Kodumanal were examined and while they were similar in cranial length and breadth to those of Adichanallur, the shape of the head was different between the two sites (Reddy and Reddy 2004).

A male skull from S. Pappinayakkanpatti site, situated at closer proximity to Kodumanal than Adichanallur, shows closer affinity to the latter. Excavation sites both at Adichanallur and Kodumanal exhibit heterogeneity characterized by a mixture of Veddid, Australoid and Mediterranean characters (Reddy and Reddy 2004).

Interestingly, no clear pattern emerges when comparing only the overall variety of types of burials at a site (Table 1.1 and Figure 1.2) but there is a definite difference in the type of burials present at each site. Here, the subjective nature of classification at each site is taken into consideration, but even accounting for that there does seem to be a very clear difference between each site. In a stable society, less of the deceased member's actual/real wealth is deposited in the tomb. In other words, fewer and fewer of the goods actually used, worn or habitually consumed in life were deposited in the tomb/consumed in the pyre (Childe 1945). It is difficult to base any study of the economy solely on the grave goods found at the burial sites but some basic ideas can be derived from grave goods.

This is implied by what is seen in the archaeological evidence (Tables 1.1 and 1.2) the burials do not seem to reveal a very strict framework. In order to understand the IA-EH burials and their regional context better, reports from excavated and explored sites in coastal and inland Tamil Nadu were compared. The division of these zones is based on geomorphologic data and previous studies. Sen (2002) mentions a matter of controversy raised by different authorities: the distance inland to which the coastal plain extended. He further talks about Ahmad's (1972) view of basing the coastal zone demarcation on the melting down of the Pleistocene glaciations resulting from the eustatic rise of sea level by about 50 meters, thus implying ingression of seal level. Sen (2002) further assigns the marine transgression to 30 kms inland in the case of the Circar coast, more than 100 kms along the Gangetic plain, 50 kms inland in case of the Coromandel coast and more than 100 kms in case of deltas. Herz and Garrison (1998) discuss the potential of coastal zones for hunting and gathering societies, due to the abundance of resources and raw material within short distances, as well as water transport such as sea, rivers and lakes for contact with others.

The different excavated burial sites imply the opposite in fact: a more adaptable/variable system. The geographic, economic and cultural divisions that have been spoken of in the literature may well reflect on localized differentiation. If these differences that are spoken of were geographic rather than geomorphic divisions, the burials of the coastal region should reflect more singularity. Instead they seem far more plural; this preliminary conclusion is however subject to available information from archaeological excavation previously conducted. When comparing the different type of burials of inland and coastal sites, it also seems obvious that the variety of typology found in coastal sites does not seem to exist with inland excavated sites (Tables 1.1 and 1.3).

A number of habitation sites have been excavated including Kancheepuram, Uraiyur, Appukallu, Perur, Kudikadu, T.Kallupatti, Adiyamankottai, Kambarmedu, Palur, Maligaimedu,, Tiruverkadu, Malyampatti, Thirukkoyilur, and having iron implements and Black and Red Ware pottery, with various phases of occupation spreads over Tamil Nadu (Sridhar 2004, Shetty 2003a, Shetty 2003b, Kasinathan and Majeed 1996, Ghosh 1989 IAR 69-70, IAR 70-71, IAR 71-72, IAR 74-75, IAR 75-76, IAR 83-84, IAR 87-88, IAR 88-89, IAR 89-90, IAR 92-93, IAR 95-96, IAR 99-00).

Grave goods vary in quantity, be it beads, pottery, iron or bronze implements. The available information being kept in mind, this does seem to reflect a certain amount of flexibility in burial customs. The surface morphology of burial types also differ; again, in some instances in spite of the similar availability of raw material. It does reflect a larger variety of burial types. Underwater exploration has also revealed submerged land off the coast of Tranquebar, presently 8 m under water. This suggests that the sea has encroached upon the land (Tripati 1993). Shell artifacts have been found at Sanur, Perumbair and Odugattur (14 kms from Vellore, North Arcot district): 10 shell objects (circular discs and long barrel shaped beads) from Odugattur, 6 shell objects from Perumbair

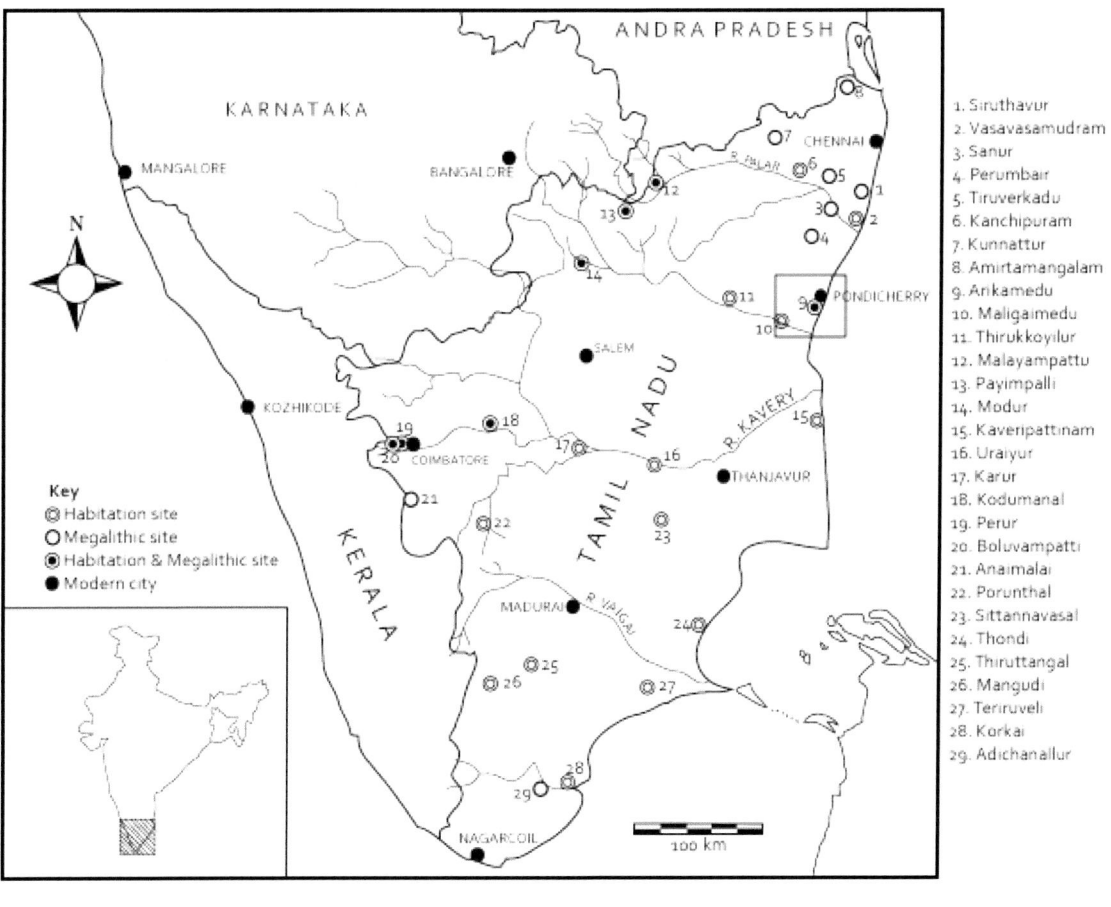

FIGURE 1.1 MAP SHOWING EXCAVATED SITES IN TAMIL NADU (MAP PREPARED BY KELLY G AND HARICHARAN S. 2010).

(conch shells, circular discs, barrel shaped longish beads) and 17 shell objects (circular discs and beads and conch) from Sanur (Banerjee and Soundararajan 1959). Though these sites are closer to the coast than other inland sites in Tamil Nadu, they are far enough inland to suggest a certain amount of trading. Among the grave goods from excavated IA-EH sites, fish hooks were also found at Tangal, Chengalpattu district, of Tamil Nadu (Hunt 1924, Deo 1985). This again correlates with the literary evidence that describes occupational differences, yet the data available from excavated sites is not large enough to establish any pattern. It is known from literary evidence that excarnation and cremation happened side by side at the same site (Srinivasan 1946, Gururaja Rao 1972, Leshnik 1972, Narasimhaiah 1980). The relationship between burying, cremating and excarnating the dead is a complex one, which intensified around 1000 BCE onwards, a date generally held to herald the Iron Age (Childe 1945).

Another concept in this ideology is that cremation encourages a belief in an afterlife rather different from burials, which maintain greater continuity with the mundane. The reduction of the human body to a handful of ashes may have required, by way of a counterpoint, a focus on the disembodied soul and its continual reincarnation (Thapar 1994). This is another example of an evolving society, different burial practices and an increase in complexity of the society at this period is corroborated by the *Sangam* literature. The relationship between cremation and burial and the simultaneous prevalence or precedence of one over the other is interesting (Codrington 1930, Crooke 1899). Crooke (1899) brings attention to not only the tribal and ethnographic information regarding the precedence of burial over cremation in India, but also differential treatment to certain people of that society, such as young children, priests or headmen.

The bones found in the IA-EH burials are inexplicably in various states of completeness and disarticulation (Codrington 1930). Gururaja Rao (1972) states that a majority of the Indian burials follow the example of the skeletal remains from Sanur: they are post excarnation secondary burials. The *Sangam* literature talks of various forms of disposal, including cremation, burial, and excarnation, yet the reasoning for the choice made is not explained in terms of social, economic or cultural factors (Srinivasan 1946). An overview of the burials excavated shows everything from near complete skeletal remains (Perambair — Table 1.2) to very few bones (Suttukeni — Table 1.2). At Tiruvakkarai, South Arcot district, the burials excavated revealed no skeletal remains and the burials, besides being loosely packed, also had a disturbed appearance. The only other site where no bones were found was at Gaurimedu near Pondicherri (Table 1.2). The excavators at Tiruvakkarai also describe the burial pits as shallow, the cairn packing measuring around 10-15 cms in thickness (IAR 84-85).

Here again the sample size and lack of information makes interpreting this anomaly difficult. More work in this respect in terms of excavation, survey and inter disciplinary methods would prove very valuable (Mohanty and Selvakumar 2002). Estimates, especially from the IA-EH burials of Karnataka and Andhra Pradesh, based on excavated megaliths suggest that individual monuments contain an average of c. 2.3 individuals (Brubaker 2001). Even were the number of known cemeteries and monuments doubled or tripled, the figures derived clearly could not account for the entire population of a period that spanned a millennium or more in some areas (Brubaker 2008). However, considering some of the burials are secondary burials with very few diagnostic remains, and other burials are non sepulchral, making any estimation of the population dynamics with respect to the IA-EH burials is difficult.

The *Sangam* people believed in life after death and they worshipped heroes; the *nadukal* was planted in memory of the dead and *virakal* for those who died in battle. A number of steps leading to the ceremonial/ritualistic practices carried out before, during and after the laying of a hero stone are described not only in later texts but also in earlier ones like the *tolkapiyar* (Vanamamalai 1975, Rajan 2000). While hero stones themselves are different from the IA-EH burials, it is probably the closest ideology we have in comparison to that of the IA-EH burials, besides the ethnographic work that has been collected. This may throw some light on the ritualistic aspect but it does not in any way explain if there existed any difference between the communities.

The only noticeable aspect of all the burials is that there seems no evident correlation between proximity of two sites, the grave goods and the type of burial. Interesting triads of burials sites are the ones excavated at Suttukeni, Muttrapaleon and Gaurimedu. While the latter two are urn burials, Suttukeni (Tables 1.1 and 1.2) has urn burials, cist burials, cairn circle and cist with circle. However, Leshnik (1972) also brings attention to the possibility that agricultural work may have resulted in the removal of the stone appendage from the surface. Similarly, there does not seem much of a correlation between the grave goods either. Gaurimedu is remarkably conspicuous by the absence of iron implements or Black and Red Ware. Leshnik (1972), Allchin and Allchin (1982) again hypothesize that it could be of an earlier period, and that the pottery from this burial resembles Brahmagiri rather than Muttrapaleon. At both Suttukeni and Perumbair, bronze bracelets have been among the grave goods, which, considering the marked lack of variety of grave goods seems a peculiar coincidence. Though the tables (Tables 1.1 and 2) provide some insight into these observations, more in-depth analysis of excavated material and more excavations are required before any kind of hypothesis can be developed.

Further north on the Tamil Nadu coast are the sites of Sanur, Kunnatur and Amrithamangalam. Amrithamangalam is different as it has only urn burial but the former two are similar in having most of the different types of burials (Tables 1.1 and 1.2). There also seems to be some similarities in the fact that the grave goods of Kunnatur and Sanur appear to be along the same lines, with the only differences being that Sanur appears to be richer in variety of beads, and that Kunnatur had a settlement site associated with the burial site (Leshnik 1972, Moorti 1994).

Another way of exploring possibilities would be to classify sites based on the *tinai*, in order to look at the artifacts and typological variations of burials at various excavated habitation and burial sites from northern Tamil Nadu. However the results of this analysis are limited by the lack of enough information from excavated sites. Yet this does show some variation in material evidence from sites located in different landscapes, whether this can be attributed to the *tinai* or not is debatable (Haricharan and Keerthi 2014). The archaeological evidence points to a fluid cultural, economic and social practice when it comes to disposal of the dead. This is mirrored in the literature as well. Despite the lack of any conclusive results, this study attempts to elucidate that the *Sangam* period was complex and earlier ideas of dividing Tamil Nadu on broad regional basis need revision. More site-specific study, using scientific methods as well as the *Sangam* literature in confluence with each other, will help in the understanding of the IA-EH period better.

1.8 CHRONOLOGY OF TAMIL NADU IA-EH BURIALS

More than fifty ^{14}C dates are available so far for IA-EH sites all over India broadly falling within the range of the late second millennium BCE to the early centuries of the Christian era (Sundara 1979, Deo 1985, Possehl 1994, Moorti 1994, Mohanty and Selvakumar 2002). In Tamil Nadu, dates from the excavated IA-EH burial sites such as Paiyampalli (North Arcot district) and Adichannallur (near Tirunelvelli) (Table 1.1, Table 1.4) reveal that the two sites were in use from 640±105 BCE (charred grain) until 1150±100 CE (wood), respectively. Agrawal et al (1964) stated that the dates from Adichannallur are not in agreement with the archaeologically accepted ages. Similarly, at Veerapatti district, Madurai, charcoal was dated from IA-EH burials but the dates were of a modern period (IAR 94-95). It is evident that the dates from the northern megaliths of Tamil Nadu (Paiyampalli) and those from southern Tamil Nadu (Adichannallur) are distinctively of different periods. However, due to the lack of well dated IA-EH sites in Tamil Nadu, no proper understanding of this chronology has been possible (Sinopoli 2002). The IA-EH burials of Karnataka and Andhra Pradesh are dated as far back as 1400 BCE to 500 BCE (Gururaja Rao 1972, Narasimhaiah 1980, Moorti 1994, Bauer et al 2007, Brubaker 2008). This also shows that there is a need for more scientific and precise dating of the IA-EH burials. 781 radiocarbon dates were used in the Menorca, Spain, megaliths to understand the significance of the typologically different burials on the island through their chronology (Gili et al 2006). The Cova des C`arritx in Menorca, a cave accidentally closed in 800 BCE and reopened in 1995, had a number of very well preserved skeletal remains and dating of this has shown that the cave was in use over many generations by closely related members of a social unit for over 600 years.

1.9 TYPOLOGY OF THE BURIALS

Among the megaliths around the world, the generally described architectural forms are menhirs (standing stones), dolmens (stone "table" or stone "house"; usually a rectangular space formed by big rock slices with or without an entrance passage and a barrow above), cromlechs (stone circles), alignments (rows with large stones) and cyclopic buildings (walls, temples, fortresses, etc.) (Kostov

Site/Type of Burial	Urn	Cist	Dolmenoid Cist	Cairn Circle	DolmenoidCist with circle	Cist with circle	Simple lined burial with sarcophagus with stone slab
Kunnathur			✓	✓		✓	✓
Sanur			✓	✓	✓	✓	✓
Amirthamangalam	✓						
Perumbair				✓			
Southykeny	✓	✓		✓		✓	
Muttrapaleon	✓						
Gaurimedu	✓						
Thiruvakkarai	✓			✓			
Siruthavoor	✓	✓	✓	✓	✓	✓	

*Source: IAR 1954-55, 1956-1957, 1984-1985, Krishnaswami and Saran 1955-1956, Krishnaswami and Saran 1956-1957, Krishnaswami and Saran 1957-1958, Banerjee and Soundararajan. 1959, Gururaja Rao 1972, Leshnik 1972, Leshnik 1974, Narasimhaiah 1980, 1985-1986, Rajan 1997, Rajan 2000

TABLE 1.1 CORRELATION BETWEEN SITES AND TYPE OF BURIAL OF COASTAL SITES IN TAMIL NADU

Site	Pottery	Metal / stone implements	Jewellery	Bones
Kunnathur	Black, Red, Black and Red	Iron: flat Celts, knives, daggers, iron spike, sword, spear head, horse bit, nails, chisel, adze, coil bracelets. Copper belts, bowls	Terracotta beads	Fragments, skull and long bone
Sanur	Black Ware, Red (slip and dull-terracotta) Ware, Black and Red Ware, Graffiti	Spear, tanged knife, bar with pointed tip and socketed end, horse bits, hook, wedge, sickle, arrowhead, scraper and chisel granite and quartzite pestle	terracotta beads, shell beads, discs, carnelian beads conch shells	skulls, disarticulated teeth
Amirthamangalam	Black and Red Ware	Few iron objects		Uncalcified skeletal remains including skull and teeth
Perumbair	Fine Black and Red Ware, Black Ware, Red Ware	iron arrowhead and blade, stone and iron implements, stone quern	bone and shell ornaments, bronze bracelet	one complete skeletal remains and disarticulated skull, jawbone and long bone, maybe different people
Suttukeni	Black, Red, Black and Red Ware	sickle, wedge, single edged knife and sword fragments, bronze mirror, vases, bells and curious objects	gold beads, glass beads, etched carnelian beads and gold jewellery	Few bones
Muttrapaleon	Black Ware, Red Ware, Black and Red Ware	sickle, wedge, double edged knife, sword, lances, javelin head (some iron implements have traces of wood)		some fragmentary bones — uncalcified — in some burials
Gaurimedu	Neolithic-like pottery	Stone axes	Bronze bracelet with trumpet ends	
Thiruvakkarai	Black and Red and Coarse Red			

*Source: IAR 1954-1955, 1956-1957, 1984-85, 1985-1986, Krishnaswami and Saran 1955-1956, Krishnaswami and Saran 1956-1957, Krishnaswami and Saran 1957-1958, Banerjee and Soundararajan. 1959, Gururaja Rao 1972, Leshnik 1972, Leshnik 1974, Narasimhaiah 1980, Rajan 1997, Rajan 2000

TABLE 1.2 CORRELATION BETWEEN SITE AND ARTIFACT EXCAVATED OF COASTAL SITES IN TAMIL NADU

2008). Generally speaking, urn burials with or without stone appendage are universal in all districts of Tamil Nadu and Kerala with a concentration in the delta ends where the availability of the stone is meager (Rajan 2000). Rajan (2000) states that dolmen or cists are found extensively in mountainous regions where pastoral economy was prevalent.

The *topikkal* (hat stone) and *kodaikkal* (umbrella stone) are found on the western coast (Rajan 2000). Rajan (2000) discusses a particular poem in *Manimekala* (a post *Sangam* literature), which describes the great necropolis port city of *Puhar* or *Kaverippattinam* where different types of burial methods or types such as *suduvor, iduvor, todu-kuli paduppar* (cists or cellars) and *tal vayin adaipor* (burial urn with inverted lid) are all carried out in the same burial site. Clearly while regional variation is present, there seem to be no strict boundaries that differentiate the type of burials. Some sites may have only a single type of burial, yet others have many types, signifying that in order to understand typological significance just classifying or tabulating site and typology is not enough.

Rajan (2000) also then says that it is possible from the literary evidence that the urn burials were largely for natural deaths while the cist burials where for those that were hailed heroes, dying in cattle raids. His major support for this theory is that the poems talk of kings also being buried in urn, in many ways implying no class differences attributed to typological choice. Again the literary evidence should be correlated with archaeological evidence to prove this as it may be purely more poetic to describe a king as one who believed in equality, or an anomaly. Rajan (2000) highlights earlier *Sangam* poem references to *idukau* (burial grounds practicing exposure or excarnation) and the later references to *sudukadu* or *imam* (cremation or lord Yama). This indicates the

Site/ Type of Burial	Urn	Cist	Dolmenoid Cist	Cairn Circle	Dolmenoid Cist with circle	Cist with circle	Simple lined burial with sarcophagus with stone slab	Menhir
Sittannavasal	✓					✓		
Kodumanal	✓	✓				✓		✓
Tiruverkadu	✓	✓				✓		✓
Paiyampalli				✓				
T. Kallupatti	✓							
Appukallu				✓				
Odugattur		✓				✓		
Adichanallur	✓							

Source: IAR A-Review 1954-55, 1956-57, 1984-85, 1985-1986, Krishnaswami and Saran 1955-1956, Krishnaswami and Saran 1956-1957, Krishnaswami and Saran 1957-1958, Banerjee and Soundararajan 1959, Gururaja Rao 1972, Leshnik 1972, Leshnik 1974, Narasimhaiah 1980, Rajan 1997, Rajan 2000

TABLE 1.3 CORRELATIONS BETWEEN SITES AND TYPE OF BURIAL OF INLAND SITES IN TAMIL NADU

possibility of some chronological change from burial to cremation. Rajan (1991, 1993, 1994) has elaborated on existing classification and he uses the following classification and parameters:

- Cairn circle (height of cairn packing is dependent on nature of burial and terrain to an extent):
    a. Cairn circle entombing cist burial
    b. Cairn circle entombing urn burial
    c. Cairn circle with double circle entombing cist burial
    d. Cairn circle with menhir
    e. Cairn circle entombing sarcophagus
- Cist (including transcepted cist burial)
- Urn burials and Sarcophagus type of burial
- Menhir
- Dolmen:
    f. Simple dolmen
    g. Dolmen encircled by single or multiple slab circles
    h. Dolmen with passage
- Dolmenoid cist
    Rajan (1991) further describes a dolmenoid cist as having the following features:
    i. Shorter in height (approx 1metre or less)
    j. Capstone placed either on rubble or boulders instead of orthostats (even if slabs are used, it consists of more than one irregular slab on each side)
    k. Three sides are closed and the remaining side is kept wide open
    l. Devoid of any porthole

1.10 PREVIOUS CLASSIFICATIONS OF MEGALITHIC BURIALS

The above table (Table 1.5) shows that the classification of burial types has been difficult, largely due to regional differences. For example, Gururaja (1972) included alignments and avenues under menhirs, and Rajan (1994) (Kongu), used transected cist and cist with passage under the cist burial types. However, the typological classification done by the above authors is based on the region in which they have worked: Rajan et al's (2009) classification is based on exploration and excavation of north Arcot, Dharmapuri district, Coimbatore region etc., while Narasimaiah (1980) concentrated on northern Tamil Nadu (Payampalli), Andhra Pradesh etc. However, Krishnaswami (1949), who made the first attempt at classification of IA-EH burials, takes into account regional as well as overall differences in megaliths. His classification of the Chengalpattu megaliths gives all above rounded "rude" stone structures as Dolmenoid cist, naming them as D1 and D2, Cairn circle with urn burials, sarcophagi. He highlights that the occurrence of sarcophagi is restricted to the coastal northern Tamil Nadu region, and clarifies the typology of Pudukottai, Adichanallur, Kerala (Cochin) and north eastern Indian megaliths.

Sample No	Place Name	Date	Calibrated dates	Site and Burial types
TF- 987	Korkai	810±95 BCE (Wood)	Cal BCE 906 (818) Cal 795	IA-EH Port site
			Cal BCE 1005 (818) Cal 558	
TF 823	Paiyampalli	640±105 BCE (Charred Grain)	Cal BCE 800 (764, 614, 606) 410	IA-EH
			Cal BCE 835 (764, 614, 606) 390	
TF 826		215±100 BCE Charcoal)	Cal BCE 333 (102) Cal AD 9	
			Cal BCE 381 (102) Cal AD 115	

(Source: IAR 65-66, IAR 69-70, Possehl 1994)

TABLE 1.4 DATES FROM PREVIOUSLY EXCAVATED IA-EH SITES

Type of Burial	K.P. Rao	K. Rajan	B.Narasimhaiah	Gururaja Rao	Allchin and Allchin	Sundara	K.R.Srinivasan and N.R.Banerjee	V.D.Krishnaswami
Transected Cist with passage			✓			✓		
Rock cut chambers		✓		✓				✓
Cist burial	✓	✓			✓	✓		✓
Port hole cist						✓	✓	✓
Dolmen (with circle of slabs)		✓						
Dolmen		✓					✓	✓
Dolmen with passage		✓						
Dolmenoid Cist	✓	✓	✓	✓		✓	✓	
Sarcophagus	✓	✓	✓			✓	✓	✓
Menhir		✓	✓	✓		✓		✓
Slab circle		✓						
Double circle		✓				✓		
Stone circle		✓	✓	✓		✓	✓	✓
Barrow						✓	✓	✓
Cairn								✓
Cairn circle		✓	✓	✓	✓	✓		
Circle with Menhirs		✓						
Cairn circle with capstone				✓				
Urn burial	✓	✓	✓			✓	✓	✓
Pit burial	✓	✓			✓	✓		
Anthropogenic figurine		✓						
Hood stone								✓
Hat stone								✓
Hood stones and Hat stones					✓			
Stone alignments						✓		
Rock cut chambers						✓	✓	
Clan ossuary								✓
Cromlech								✓
Stone seats								✓
Topikal							✓	✓
Avenue								✓
Alignment								✓

(Source: Krishnaswami 1949 Gururaja Rao 1972, Sundara 1979, Narasimhaiah 1980, Allchin and Allchin 1983, Rao 1988, Rajan 1991, Rajan 1993, Rajan 1994, Moorti 1994)

TABLE 1.5 CLASSIFICATION OF BURIALS PUT FORWARD BY SEVERAL ARCHAEOLOGISTS

Two very different approaches to the classification system however are by Sundara (1979), who divides the burials into chambers and non-chambers, and Moorti (1994), who divides the burials into sepulchral and non-sepulchral. However without excavation or firm establishment of any type as non-sepulchral, it is difficult to effectively use this system at all sites. The division of burials into chamber and non-chamber however is interesting in that it tries to think outside the nomenclature already given. Dikshit (1969), however finds Krishnaswami's (1949) classification problematic in that it does not distinguish cist from dolmen, but instead uses dolmenoid cist. Dikshit (1969) further advocates the Montelian system of three broad classifications, as this helps understand the correlation between typology and chronology of different burial types, Using this logic, he believes the classification of burials into cist and dolmen type is effective as this is not only typological but also a chronological differentiation, as the cist burials are dated later than the dolmen. Table 1.5 also shows that the basic types are the same: dolmen, cist, circle, without stone appendage, yet the sub divisions are where the variations occur. The large number of burial types and extent would suggest that such variations are due to raw material or social or cultural divisions. Sundara (1979) also states that post depositional process may change the appearance of the burials, and unless these processes are considered, typology is harder to interpret.

When a site contained more than one type of burial, each type occupied a separate portion within the complex as noticed by Mungilpudur and Pachchihanapalli (Rajan 1993). It has been noticed that in many sites chambers in all three states (cist, dolmenoid-cist or dolmen) or exclusively in either of the states, or in the last two states but segregated from each other, are found. This is exemplified by the passage chambers in all the states in North Karnataka, dolmens in the Palani hills, cist circles in Brahmagiri and dolmens and dolmenoid cists in Hire-Benkal (Sundara 1979). Though geological conditions of the spots where the chambers are erected appear to be the reasons for the different states of the erections in north Karnataka, they do not hold true in the case of others (Sundara 1979). The reasons for such preferences appear to be more cultural than environmental: a problem for further study (Sundara 1979).

The cairn circle entombing cist burial generally was raised (or lowered) 2-3 m above; those entombing the urns are 30-50 cm raised above ground or below. Rajan et al (2009) infers that the Palar basin is influenced by the cairn circles from Pennaiyar river region, the stone circle and other stone variety of burials from eastern and western parts, respectively, of Chittoor district, Andhra Pradesh, and the dolmenoid cists either originated here or from Chengalpattu where they are found in vast numbers. However, a large number of the theories are based on a general comparison of surface typology of the burials, not exploring in-depth any specific aspects of the burials like the spatial and temporal behavior of these burials.

1.11 THE IA-EH SITE-SIRUTHAVOOR

Siruthavoor has cairn circle, dolmen, dolmen with circle, dolmenoid cist, cist, cist with circle and urn burials. The chronology and typological analysis of the burials is integral to further understanding the origin and distribution of IA-EH burials. Thus considering present theories and previous studies conducted, a site such as Siruthavoor provides a unique opportunity to understand the relationship between different types of burials and their chronology.

The study of IA-EH burials has a long history (Mohanty and Selvakumar 2002), however, gaps still remain. The many questions raised have only multiplied, and grown more complex. The need presently is to understand IA-EH burials and how they fit into the proto history of south India. Besides typological classifications, which may be the key to understanding any society, economic or other differences of that society need further analysis. Since the IA-EH burials are very much a part of the landscape, which is subject to change over a period of time, the burials have to be studied in that context. Dating the IA-EH burials is also important as we need to further understand the chronology to verify its impact of typology.

Chapter 2
Siruthavoor: An Iron Age-Early Historic site

2.1 INTRODUCTION

Siruthavoor is located in Kancheepuram district of Tamil Nadu nearly 45 kms South of Chennai (Figure 2.1). This site is 5 kms southeast of Thiruporur, 15 kms northwest of Thirukkalukundram in the south and nearly 8 kms inland. A 10 kms radius around Siruthavoor was surveyed for evidence of IA-EH burials and habitation using information from reports of recorded sites, toposheet and satellite images. The present day village of Siruthavoor spreads over 3 sq kms area, and the IA-EH site falls mostly within the village limits, however some of it falls within an area protected by the Tamil Nadu forest department. The area over which the IA-EH burials are located is bounded by the Siruthavoor lake towards the south, and a larger hillock of around 31 msl height towards the north, with a smaller hillock (below 15 msl) of not much elevation (Figure 2.1). The second hillock is made up of a few boulders and situated between the lake and larger hillock.

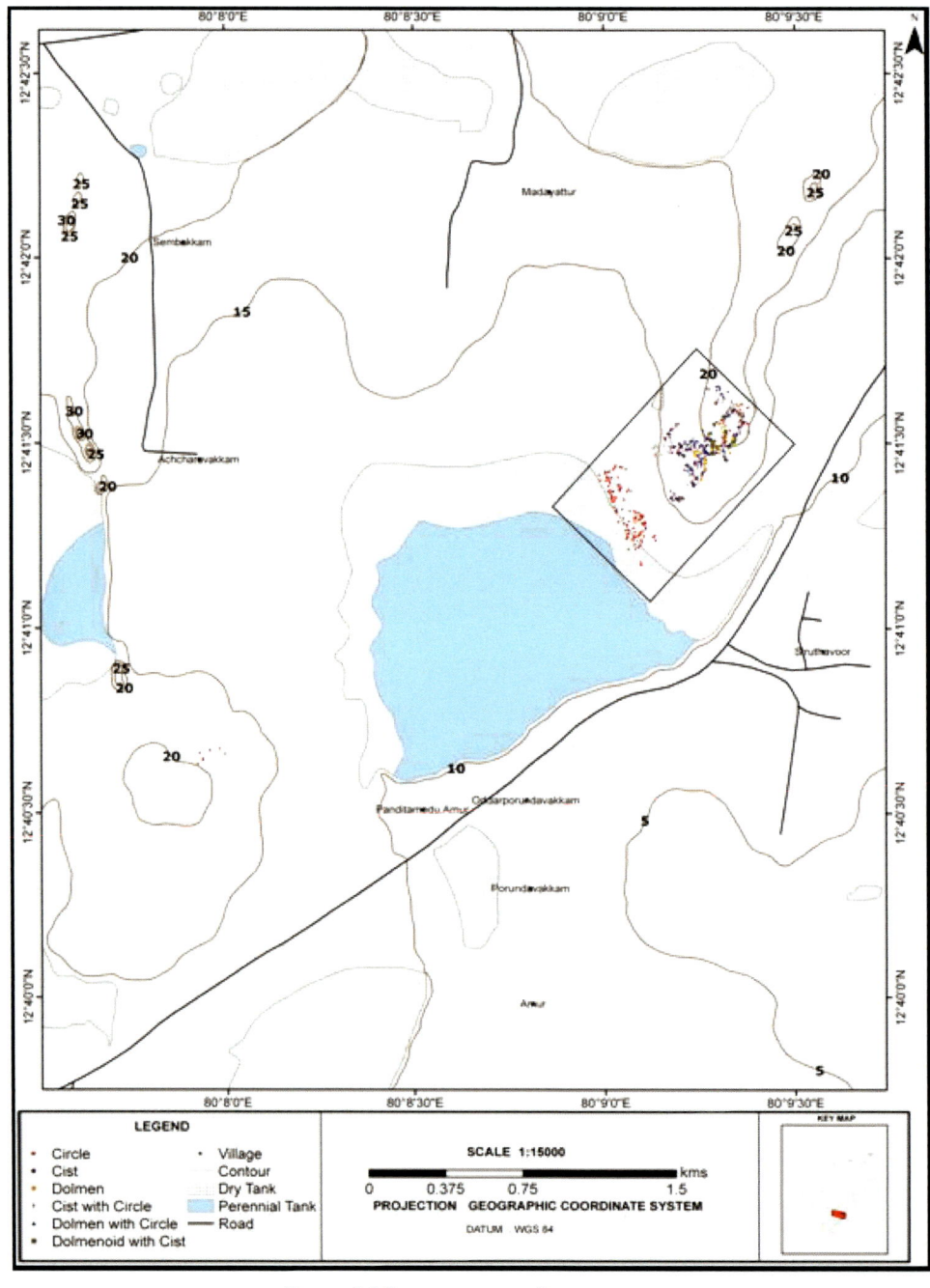

FIGURE 2.1 THE STUDY AREA: SIRUTHAVOOR

CHAPTER 2 SIRUTHAVOOR: AN IRON AGE-EARLY HISTORIC SITE

FIGURE 2.2 STUDY AREA SHOWING 1. ENCROACHMENT, 2. DOLMEN WITH CIRCLE AND 3. SIRUTHAVOOR LAKE

2.2 GEOMORPHOLOGY

According to Subramaniam and Selvan (2001) the prominent geomorphic units identified around the study area are i) Chengalpattu-Thirukkalukundram Surface (Erosional) with monadknocks of charnockites at Pallavaram, Thirukkalukundram, Muttukadu ii) Palar River bed (fluvial) and iii) Mamallapuram surface (coastal beach). Siruthavoor falls within the first category, the very gradual slope towards the south-southwest results in the collection of water into a lake found bordering the archaeological site (2.1). The elevation of the area ranges from 217 m amsl (Thirukkalukundram) to rocky waste land with boulders having an elevation as low as 20 msl (Kunnapattu). The major part of the area is characterised by an undulating topography with innumerable depressions, which are used as irrigation tanks (Anon 2007).

The closest major rivers in the area are the Palar and Cheyyar, the Palar lies 20 Km Southwest of the study area. The drainage pattern in general of these rivers is sub-dendritic and radial. All the rivers are seasonal and carry substantial flows during NE monsoon period. Palar, a major river course, which drains this district originates from Western Ghats in Karnataka state, and discharges in to the Bay of Bengal near Pudupattinam. The Cheyyar, a tributary of Palar originates from the Jawadu Hills of Tiruvannamalai district. It has a northeasterly flow in Kancheepuram district and confluences with the Palar near Pazhaiyaseevaram (Anon 2007). The present day geomorphology of the study area is vastly altered due to anthropogenic factors such as sand mining, which creates an increase in the erosion and sedimentation of soil through aeolian and water erosion.

2.3 GEOLOGY

The geology of the area is represented by Archaean to Precambrian crystalline formations overlain by Mesozoic and Tertiary sedimentary rocks. The older deposits are unconformably overlain by sandy and clayey soils of Recent to Sub-Recent ages (Rajmohan and Elango 2005). The Charnockites occur as monadknocks and pediments with different weathering pattern while the Quaternary

FIGURE 2.3 EXPOSED STATIGRAPHIC SECTIONS AT SIRUTHAVOOR

Geology	Time
Red soil, Lateritic pebbles and gravels,	Recent –Sub-recent
Laterite-saprolite horizon	Late Neogene-Early Quaternary period
Charnockite, Granite, intruded by Quartz vein	Archaean –Precambrian

Source: Compiled and updated from Subramanian and Selvan (2001)

TABLE 2.1 STRATIGRAPHY OF THE SIRUTHAVOOR SITE

deposits occur either as regolith over the pediments or as valley fills (Achyuthan et al 2000, Subramanian and Selvan 2001).

The crystalline formations are charnockite, granite gneiss and ultra basic rocks. The crystalline charnockite and granite gneiss of Archaean age are intruded by amphibolites, dolerite dykes and occasionally by quartz and pegmatite veins (Rajmohan and Elango 2005, Sen 2002). The charnockite is overlain by red sand or clay which at Siruthavoor has undergone lateritisation and the exposed boulders and rock features show onion peel weathering layers (Table 2.1 and Figure 2.3). The tectonic history of the study area is represented by the north-south trending fault that traverses through the costal part of the area. Relative uplift has been mainly along reactivated NNE-SSW and NNW–SSE and N-S trending structure (Achyuthan 1996, Achyuthan et al 2000, Subramanian and Selvan 2001, Sen 2002).

2.4 SOIL TYPES

The soil type is regur and alluvial soils. Soils here are technically classified as Psamments-Tropepts and Ustalfs-Tropepts (Anon 2006). The soil type is alluvial and sandy soil. Soils here are technically classified as Psamments-Fluvents and Psamments-Tropepts (Anon 2006) The stratigraphic section at Siruthavoor shows a short and shallow weathering profile, with an intermediate layer of lateritisation and overlain by a top yellowish brown (2.5 YR 7/6 and sandy silt unit (Figure 2.3).

2.5 CLIMATE AND RAINFALL

Kancheepuram district generally experiences hot and humid climatic conditions. High relative humidity between 58 and 84% prevail through out the year, being maximum in the morning and minimum in the evening. Higher rates of relative humidity are observed between November and January i.e., 83 to 84%. In the months of June, the humidity is lower i.e., around 58% (Anon 2006). The climate of Tamil Nadu is tropical monsoon type and the study site Siruthavoor experiences the same climatic conditions. The minimum and maximum temperature in this region on an average is 20°C and 37°C (Anon 2007).

The district receives the rain under the influence of both southeast and northeast monsoons but intensely during the north east monsoon (during October and November months) (Achyuthan 1996). Most of the precipitation occurs during the northeast monsoon period in the form of cyclonic storm caused due to the depressions in Bay of Bengal chiefly. Rainfall during the southwest monsoon is highly erratic and any summer rains is negligible. The normal annual rainfall over the area varies from 1,105 mm to 1,214 mm, with an average annual precipitation of 1,023 mm. (Anon 2006, Anon 2007). The climate is classified as dry sub-humid with an attenuated degree of aridity (Sprangers and Balasubramaniyam 1978).

2.6 VEGETATION

The vegetation is mainly of the tropical dry evergreen type and over 350 species of plants has been found including trees, shrubs, climbers, herbs and grasses. Agricultural and agro pastoral activities are carried out around this area include, paddy, millet and pulses (Anon 2006). Thorny shrubs such as acacia and small trees around the archaeological site lend themselves more to pastoral activities on the site in the contemporary context, while the agricultural land is more prevalent towards the southeastern and northwestern sides of the study area.

2.7 THE IA-EH BURIALS OF SIRUTHAVOOR

The number of burials at Siruthavoor is numerous, besides also being of more than one type. During reconnaissance survey it was noted that some isolated hillocks seemed to have some significance to the typological placement of the burials (Figure 2.2). IA-EH burials are also found at Thiruporur, including dolmen, cairn circles and urn burials. This site is situated around and on the hillock within the limits of Thiruporur

Datura sp	
Family	Solanaceae
English Name	Green Thorn apple
Calotropis gigantica	
Family	Asclepiadaceae
English Name	Giant milkweed
Sida acuta	
Family	Malvaceae
English Name	Morning mallow

(After Achyuthan et al 2000).

TABLE 2.2 MAJOR PLANT VARIETIES FOUND AROUND CHENNAI

Chapter 2 Siruthavoor: An Iron Age-Early Historic site

Acacia nilotica sub sp indica	Acacia leucopholea, Willd	Acacia farnesiana Willd
Acacia ferruginea, DC	Acacia catechu Willd	Acacia horrida (L.F) Willd
Acacia sinuata (Lour)	Acacia pennata Willd	Acacia senegal Willd
	Acacia modesta Wall	

(After Achyuthan et al 2000)

TABLE 2.3 SOME VARIETIES OF ACACIA FOUND GROWING AROUND CHENNAI

township, which is a busy contemporary pilgrimage centre, Rajan et al (2009) also reports a habitation site at Thiruporur. The present day urbanization, and the proximity of the archaeological sites to Chennai are leading to large scale site destruction. Nearly 1/3rd of Siruthavoor site has been destroyed. Since 2006, exposed burials were located at the site. While this is unfortunate it made documentation a viable option, as well as the presence of intact burials for excavation, offering the opportunity for detailed study of a coastal IA-EH site of Tamil Nadu. This site was chosen for study, due to the scope of work possible (Figure 2.4).

FIGURE 2.4 LARGE AREAS OF THE SITE DESTROYED DUE TO NATURAL AND ANTHROPOGENIC ACTIVITIES

Chapter 3
Methodology

3.1 INTRODUCTION

This study incorporates field data such as intensive survey, mapping and excavation in order to understand the relationship between the spatial and temporal patterning of the IA-EH burials. The study also factors into its methodology topographic features using not only mapping, field points but also laboratory analysis such as geo-chemical and textural analysis. Optically stimulated dating of potsherds and micromorphology of pot sherds have also been carried out for Siruthavoor. The methodology adopted is graphically represented in the flow chart given below (Figure 3.1).

3.2 EXPLORATION AND EXCAVATION

The initial exploration was carried out using a topographic maps and available literature in order to locate previously explored and reported IA-EH burials sites. These include Kalvoy, Kumili, Thiruporur, Siruthavoor, Oragadam besides previously excavated sites such as Sanur, Amrithamangalam, Auroville and Arikamedu (Table 3.1.) were explored. The type of burials situated at each site was documented along with observations on their spatial patterns. Exploration around the Kancheepuram district was conducted from April 2006 onwards, during which the area area around Siruthavoor was also explored. The number and variety of burials at this site was identified. It was also obvious that the site was steadily being destroyed due to sand quarrying which in turn also accentuated other natural (erosion from fluvial activities) and anthropogenic (stone quarrying) activities. Based on these factors significant burials were chosen for excavation in order to better understand the burials, their correlation to the topography, and chronology of the burials and to collect samples for laboratory work within the available timeframe. Excavation of the site was conducted between July –September 2008, as the result of a collaborative between Department of Geology; Anna University, Chennai and Archaeological Survey of India, Chennai circle.

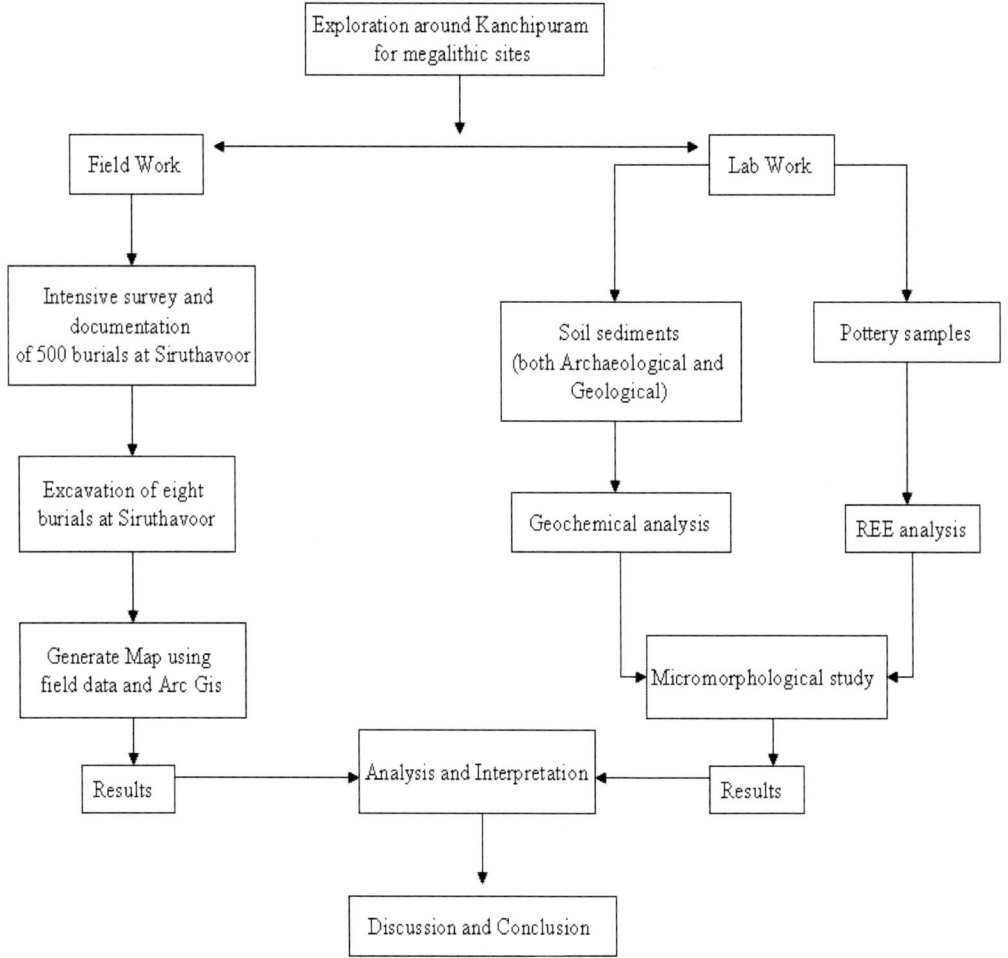

FIGURE 3.1 FLOW CHART SHOWING THE DIFFERENT METHODOLOGIES ADOPTED FOR UNDERSTANDING THE FORMATION OF THE SITE

3.3 CLASSIFICATION AND MAPPING OF DIFFERENT BURIAL TYPES

Chapter 1 has dealt with an overview of the different classification methods used in previous work carried out on IA-EH burials. Given below are the criteria and classification adopted at Siruthavoor following the rough outline of previous classification with some alterations. Previous classification system (Rajan 1991, 1993, Krishnaswami 1949) give basic burial types as cairn circle, dolmen, dolmenoid cist and cist burials, with many subdivisions. The classification carried out at Siruthavoor follows Rajan (1991, 1993) with some changes in dolmen and dolmenoid cist as given below:

Cairn Circle: The cairn circles include any burial which has been marked by a circle of stones, sometimes with cairn packing. The identification of a clear shape of any other stone structure found within the burial excludes the burial from being classified as a cairn. Any slab or stone appendage found within the circle was not taken into account as a cist unless a clear rectangular or square shape or at least two sides were visible.

Dolmen: Burials which had stone walls on four sides dressed or otherwise with a capstone on top rounded or slab like, were taken into account as a dolmen. Those which were low and could be also thought of as a dolmenoid cist were differentiated based on the height of the structure, and the occurrence of dressed or undressed slabs visible above the surface rather than like the cist lowered completely into the surface. In the case of a disturbed dolmen where the chances were that the capstone could have been anthropogenically altered or removed, careful attention to shape of base was applied. The basic types of intact dolmen at Siruthavoor, followed the pattern of having either 5 or 2 long stones as base; none of the dolmens were noticed as having 4 equally long stones on each side below the capstone. One type of burial found at Siruthavoor, having two long rounded slabs, appeared to be partially dressed, and had a monolithic or double capstone on top was classified as a dolmen. This type could not be called a cist, and appeared closer to the description of a dolmen than a cist, and thereby classified as dolmen.

Around 10 burials at Siruthavoor, also had a flush capstone, these again do not strictly follow the description of a dolmen, as specified by Rajan (1996). However due to the rough rounded stone on top and sometimes visible supporting stone underneath these capstones of very less thickness it was closer in description to a dolmen rather than a cist or dolmenoid cist. Rajan (1996) has classified this as a dolmenoid cist, Banerjee and Sounderarajan (1959) have classified it as a cist, however as the capstone used in this type of burial, resembles that of a dolmen it was considered a dolmen for the purpose of this study.

Dolmenoid cist: The main method used in the field was to limit those classified as dolmenoid cist to any burial which was low enough to clearly distinguish it from a disturbed dolmen. The burial also had to have a clearly square or swastika-like (the word swastika here is used not in a ritualistic sense) pattern/ Unlike the cist which is made often using dressed stone in order to be classified as a dolmenoid cist, the stones used were more like rough boulders, they may or may not have had a capstone originally.

Cist: Burials having four sides which were not boulder shaped like the dolmen and dolmenoid cist but had dressed stone walls, at Siruthavoor, not having an obvious capstone, like those of the dolmen, on the surface were categorised as cist burial.

Urn burials: Burials visible in the section or surface, having no associated stone appendage to mark them on the surface, except for occasion stone slabs, which were below the surface, were classified as urn burials for the purpose of this study. Care was taken to leave out any burials whose stone appendage was removed by the sand quarrying. The area where urn burials were found was segregated from the rest of the burials. Any urn burials or sarcophagi with or without a slab on it found within the parameters of the area destroyed by sand quarrying were documented but not used for the purpose of the map.

This site was then surveyed using a hand held GPS, and the location of over 500 burials was recorded along with type of burial and field observations (Figures 4.12 and 4.22) (Annexure 1). The data was then represented on a toposheet using *Arc Map 9.1* (ESRI) for the purpose of digitising the map and ENVI (Environment for Visualizing Images) 4.5 version was used for geo referencing the map in order to further analyse the spatial patterning. A contour map was created using information from satellite image of the area and toposheet 66D/2; scale1:25,000, on which the burials were located so as to understand the importance of topography on the placement of burial type within the site.

The surrounding areas were also explored for any possible habitation sites. An apsidal (*Gajaprishta*) Siva temple which has inscriptions dating to the 13th century was located. However inspite of intensive ground survey no habitation site other than the present day village has been located as yet. Five lithosections exposed at different locations within the site were recorded and sampled for textural, geochemical and mineral analyses (Figures 4.38 to 4.40).

3.4 EXCAVATION

In 2008, Ms. Sathyabhama Badhreenath, the then Superintending Archaeologist of the Archaeological Survey of India (Chennai Circle) and Dr. Hema Achyuthan, Professor, Department of Geology, Anna

University, Chennai were the Principle Investigators of the excavation conducted at Siruthavoor. I worked as a research assistant on this project, being primarily responsible for maintaining the field notes during the excavation and preparing preliminary reports for the excavation. Thus, the final report brought out by the ASI (Badhreenath 2011) utilized some of the raw data that is presented in this chapter. Out of over 500 burials, eight burials were excavated between July-September 2008 at Siruthavoor, Kancheepuram District, identified here as Burial 1-8. These are:

- Burial 1 - a cairn circle,
- Burial 2 - a pit with Sarcophagi, disturbed, with uncertain associated stone appendage,
- Burial 3 - a cist with dressed stone with a stone circle also partially disturbed.
- Burial 4 - a complete dolmen built with rough rounded stone boulders,
- Burial 5 - a complete dolmen with a stone circle,
- Burial 6 - a complete dolmenoid cist without a stone circle,
- Burial 7 - an urn burial with a capstone and
- Burial 8 - an urn burial without capstone both partially disturbed. The burials were drawn and documented during the excavation.

3.5 OSL DATING SAMPLES

Six samples of pottery were collected, which were taken from either the sarcophagi or urns, depending on what was found in the burials. Since the sarcophagi or urn was one of the main features present in each burial and to reduce the possibility of dating pottery samples which had been introduced into the burials at later stages. These samples were specifically chosen to give an estimate for the period of use of this site as an IA-EH burial site as well as the relative chronology of the burials. OSL dating was carried out at the Wadia Institute of Himalayan Geology, Dehra Dun (Table 5.26). The materials dated were the quartz grains extracted from the sarchophagi or urn sherds. The grain size ranged from 90-125 μm and the dating method was according to the SAR protocol of Murray and Wintle (2000). Using SAR-OSL, the paleodose estimation was possible from a single aliquot which means that the amount of sample required was very small, the estimate more precise and the procedure automated and rapid following Murray and Wintle (2000).

Siruthavoor, is a site with various types of IA-EH burials, and has not been dated by any scientific method. Given the available dating materials i.e. lack of organic material, OSL dating was chosen in order to establish a chronology of the burials within the site. Dating the burials from this site will help in understanding how the IA-EH burials of this region fit into the chronology of the burials in Tamil Nadu and also reveal how the site has been altered by the IA-EH builders.

3.6 TEXTURAL ANALYSIS

The sediment samples were dried at 40oC and each sample was sieved at class interval of 0.5 Φ following the method of Carver (1971). A Haver EML digital plus, sieve shaker was used, each sample was sieved for 15 minutes, at 1.5 amplitude at 15μ second intervals at the Department of Geology, Anna University, Chennai. The data was then statistically analysed using gradistat, following Folk and Ward (1957) (Tables 5.1 to 5.10). The silt and clay mixture that were collected in the washings were further analysed and classified as silt and clay fractions using the pippete method of Krumbein and Pettijohn (1938). After complete drying the sand, silt and clay were weighted and this was converted into weight percentages and plotted on a trilinear diagram following Trefethen (1950).

3.7 MICROMORPHOLOGY OF POTTERY

Thin sections of pot sherds (22) collected from the burials were studied under the petrological microscope. Thin sections were prepared on air-dried samples and impregnated following the methods of Guillore (1985). Micromorphological features were studied following Bullock et al (1985).

3.8 GEOCHEMISTRY

Sediment samples and archaeological sediments were collected for geochemical analyses to determine the major oxide, trace elements and Rare Earth Elements (REE) concentrations to understand digenetic changes after the IA-EH burials were placed within the landscape (Tables 5.11-5.25, 5.27, 5.28). Samples of archaeological sediments were collected during the excavation, the samples were collected by selective sampling at various depths. Due to the fact that Burial 1 had a balk running through the centre of the burial, with an east facing stratigraphic section and another facing west. The sediments were collected from this burial, from northern, southern, western and eastern, as well as central area of the Burial 1 from approximately the same areas at varying depths. On the eastern quadrant there were 3 layers as well as a pit, samples from each of these layers was collected. The western quadrant in contrast to the eastern quadrant which was excavated till over 70 cm in depth was only excavated as far as 40cm depth, thus fewer samples were collected from this quadrant. This burial also had four 1x1 m trenches laid on the outside of these circles, and samples were collected from these trenches as well.

Burial 2 was a disturbed burial, and very few samples were collected from this burial, and samples were collected from around the main feature of this burial, which was a sarcophagus. Burial 3 was a cist burial, and no section was retained during the excavation, and since the sediments were all reddish and similar in texture, samples were collected at varying depths again in association with the pottery as well as one sample from outside the cist, from within the cairn packing found on the eastern side outside this burial. Burials 4 and 5 were dolmen built on top of a base rock (outcrop) excavated such that the sampling was done based on proximity to artifacts. Burials 7 and 8 were urn burials, both were partially disturbed. The statigraphic section of Burial 8 had a 30 cm thick layer of redeposit sediments as the topmost layer, as a result of the construction of a road, which had also revealed these burials.

Along with the archaeological sediment samples, geological sediment samples were collected from a lithosection, at an interval of 20 cm, except for 2 samples at a depth of 70-80 cm which were collected at 10 cm interval as this layer was a transitional layer.

3.8.1 Major Oxide

The samples were also analysed for SiO_2, Al_2O_3 using Spectrophotometer (Systronics UV- Vis spectrophotometer 118) in Department of Geology, Anna University, Chennai. Elements such as Fe, Mn and trace elements Co, Cu, Cr, Fe, Pb, Mn, Ni, Zn, and Mg were analyzed using an Atomic Absorption Spectrometer, GBC 930 plus model in the Department of Geology, Anna University, Chennai. Merck standards for each element were used repeatedly for the accuracy of the analysis.

3.8.1.1 CIA

Nesbit and Young (1982) proposed the Chemical Index of Alteration (CIA) to quantify the intensity of weathering

$$CIA = \frac{Al_2O_3}{Al_2O_3 + CaO + Na_2O + K_2O} \times 100 \quad (3.1)$$

in clastic sedimentary source using molecular proportion of the oxides following the equation (3.1):

This was the method used to analyse the CIA for the samples using the major oxide results as stated above.

3.8.2 REE Analysis

Five samples of pottery collected from the excavated burials and four samples of clay, one from the Siruthavoor lake, two from nearby monsoonal rivulets, and one from a potter in Chennai as well as one sample of red coloured sediment collected from the surface near the clay sample were analysed for REE. These samples were analysed using ICPAES at the Geochemistry Laboratory, National Geophysical Research Institute, Hyderabad. SO-1 standards were used repeatedly for the accuracy of the analysis. The results obtained were normalized using the Upper Continental Crust, PAAS and Chondrite values (Taylor and McLenan 1985) at NGRI, Hyderabad

3.9 FLOTATION

For the purpose of this study, all sediment samples found within the pottery in burials such as Burial 3 where intact pottery was excavated, as well as some lithosection samples (control) were analyzed for any organic matter through floatation. After samples had been removed for textural analysis, geochemical and mineral analysis the remaining sediments were tested for organic content. Bucket flotation method was applied following Fuller and Qin (2009).

Chapter 4
Exploration and Excavation at Siruthavoor

4.1 INTRODUCTION

Of the reported megalithic site approximately less than 1% of the sites have been excavated. However there is also evidence of uneven distribution of megalithic burial sites within Tamil Nadu, Kerala, Karnataka and Andhra Pradesh and little systematic survey has been carried out (Sinapoli 2002, Mohanty and Selvakumar 2002). Conducting large scale exploration and excavation of megalithic sites is necessary, at the same time understanding each megalithic site within the context of the landscapes they are located within is also required. This chapter describes the exploration and excavation carried out at Siruthavoor.

4.2 EXPLORATION OF IA-EH BURIAL SITES AROUND SIRUTHAVOOR

The following sites were reported by Rajan et al (2009) for the area north of Palar River in Kancheepuram district, in the immediate vicinity of Siruthavoor. These sites

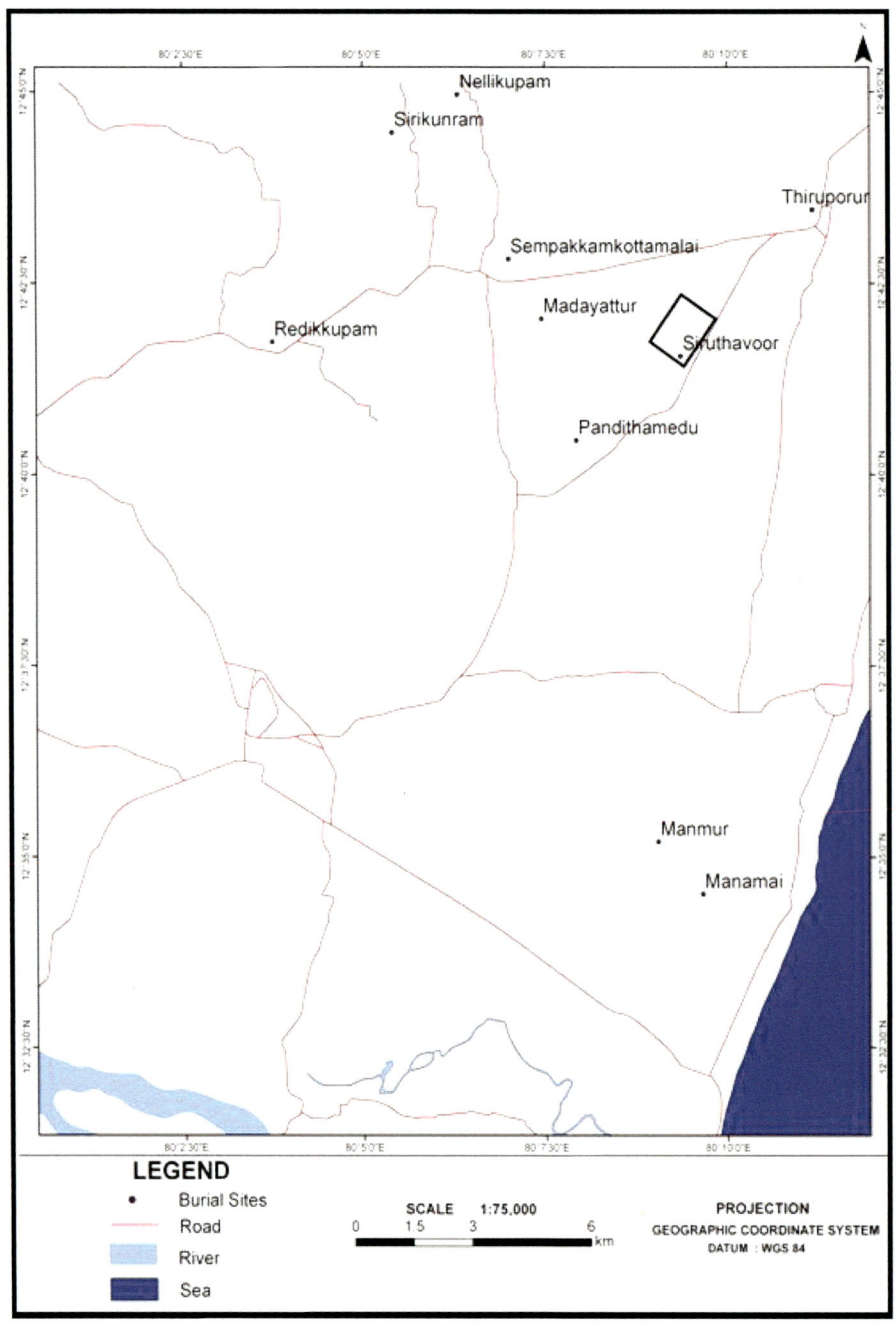

FIGURE 4.1 STUDY AREA SIRUTHAVOOR AND OTHER IA-EH SITES AROUND SIRUTHAVOOR

CHAPTER 4 EXPLORATION AND EXCAVATION AT SIRUTHAVOOR

were Reddikupam (Chengalpattu Taluk) which is reported to be having dolmen, Thiruporur (Chengalpattu Taluk) as having habitation site and cairn circle with cist, Manamai (Tirukalukundram Taluk) reported to have cairn circle with urns (Tirukalukundram Taluk), Manmur (Tirukalukundram Taluk) having Paleolithic and Early-historic habitation sites with Rouletted Ware, Nellikuppam (Chengalpattu Taluk) having Cairn circle with urns, Oragadam (Tirukalukundram Taluk) with Paleolithic tools and Sempakkamkottamalai (Chengalpattu Taluk) with dolmens (Figure 4.1.).

This study involved, analysis of satellite data, toposheets and field explorations in order to understand the IA-EH burial and habitation sites around Siruthavoor. The largest IA-EH sites that were identified were Siruthavoor, Thiruporur, Amur (referred to as Pandithamedu in toposheet 66 D/2) and Manamai (all within 10 km radius). Satellite data also shows burials near Madayathur which is a few km northeast of Siruthavoor site. At Thiruporur burial types included dolmen, with and without circle, circles, cist and urn burials and at Manamai, cairn circles and dolmen were observed. Further exploration around

FIGURE 4.2 SITE SIRUKUNRAM: CAIRN CIRCLE

FIGURE 4.3 DOLMEN WITH CURVED CAIRN CIRCLE STONES AT SIRUTHAVOOR

Oragadam revealed occurrence of Paleolithic tools and at Sirikunram a couple of cairn circles in a paddy field, but these were disturbed (Figure 4.2).

Analysing information gathered from satellite imagery as well as toposheets led to the identification and exploration of the area around village named Amur (Pandithamedu). This site south of the Siruthavoor Lake, with both sites having similar burial types. This included cairn circles, cist burials with and without circle, dolmen with and without circle and sarcophagi. The burials at Amur were not just similar to Siruthavoor in general appearance but also similar in specific typological appearance. Some of the cairn circles in both the sites had similar features such as curved or rounded tops of the stones which formed a part of the cairn circle (Figures 4.3 and 4.4). Slabs which rested on smaller boulders forming a very low type of dolmen (Figures 4.5 and 4.6) as well as dolmen with five or more stones with a huge slab on top with one side having flattened stones (Figures 4.7 and 4.8).

FIGURE 4.4 DOLMEN WITH CURVED CAIRN CIRCLE STONES AT AMUR

FIGURE 4.5 DOLMEN VERY LOW IN SIRUTHAVOOR WITH 2 LARGE SLABS AS CAPSTONE

FIGURE 4.6 DOLMEN VERY LOW IN AMUR WITH 2 LARGE SLABS AS CAPSTONE

FIGURE 4.7 DOLMEN AT AMUR WITH ANTI-CHAMBER AND LARGE FLAT BOULDER AS CAPSTONE

4.3 SPATIAL PATTERN OF BURIALS AT SIRUTHAVOOR

More than 559 burials were recorded at Siruthavoor and are presented below (Figures 4.12 to 4.22, Annexure 1). Table (4.1) represents the number and type of burials documented during the exploration.

For building these burials, two varieties of raw material were used, granitic gneiss and charnokite which are locally available (Figure 4.9).

Type of burial	Number of burials
Circle	166
Dolmen	123
Dolmen with circle	157
Cist	38
Cist with circle	57
Dolmenoid cist	18
Total	559

TABLE 4.1. INDIVIDUAL TYPE OF BURIAL AND THEIR NUMBER

FIGURE 4.8 DOLMEN AT SIRUTHAVOOR WITH ANTI-CHAMBER AND LARGE FLAT BOULDER AS CAPSTONE

Some of the features on the burials at Siruthavoor and Amur give some indication of either techniques used in building these burials (Figures 4.10 and 4.11) and post depositional anthropogenic alterations. The boulders and slabs, (especially the cap stones) of some of these burials, have square holes arranged in a line. These holes could have been used to split the boulders to extract raw material for the burials, or the result of the burials being used as a source of raw material at later periods. Rocks (2009) states that, especially during Chola period, in order to obtain raw material for

FIGURE 4.9 Gnranatic Gneiss and Charnokite used for IA-EH burials at Siruthavoor

FIGURE 4.10 CAPSTONE AT AMUR SHOWING SIGNS OF BEING SHAPED

FIGURE 4.11 CAPSTONE FROM SIRUTHAVOOR WITH A LINE OF HOLES PROBABLY FOR CUTTING OR SHAPING OF STONE

temples, the stone masons of the period, used to carve small holes with the help of chisels, aligned in a straight line and insert wooden pieces into these holes, on these wooden pieces water was poured, due to the contraction and expansion of the wooden piece cracks would develop, which was then used to break the stone.

Wheeler (1948) on the other hand describes the use of heat application and iron wedges in order to extract slabs for cist building which he also reported from the excavation of one of the megaliths at Brahmagiri. A nail/chisel like object, in a good state of preservation was a part of the surface finds at Siruthavoor, found next to a sarcophagus with a few other iron implements. However due to the fact that it was located on the surface it is difficult without further anlaysis to correlate this implement with the IA-EH structures.

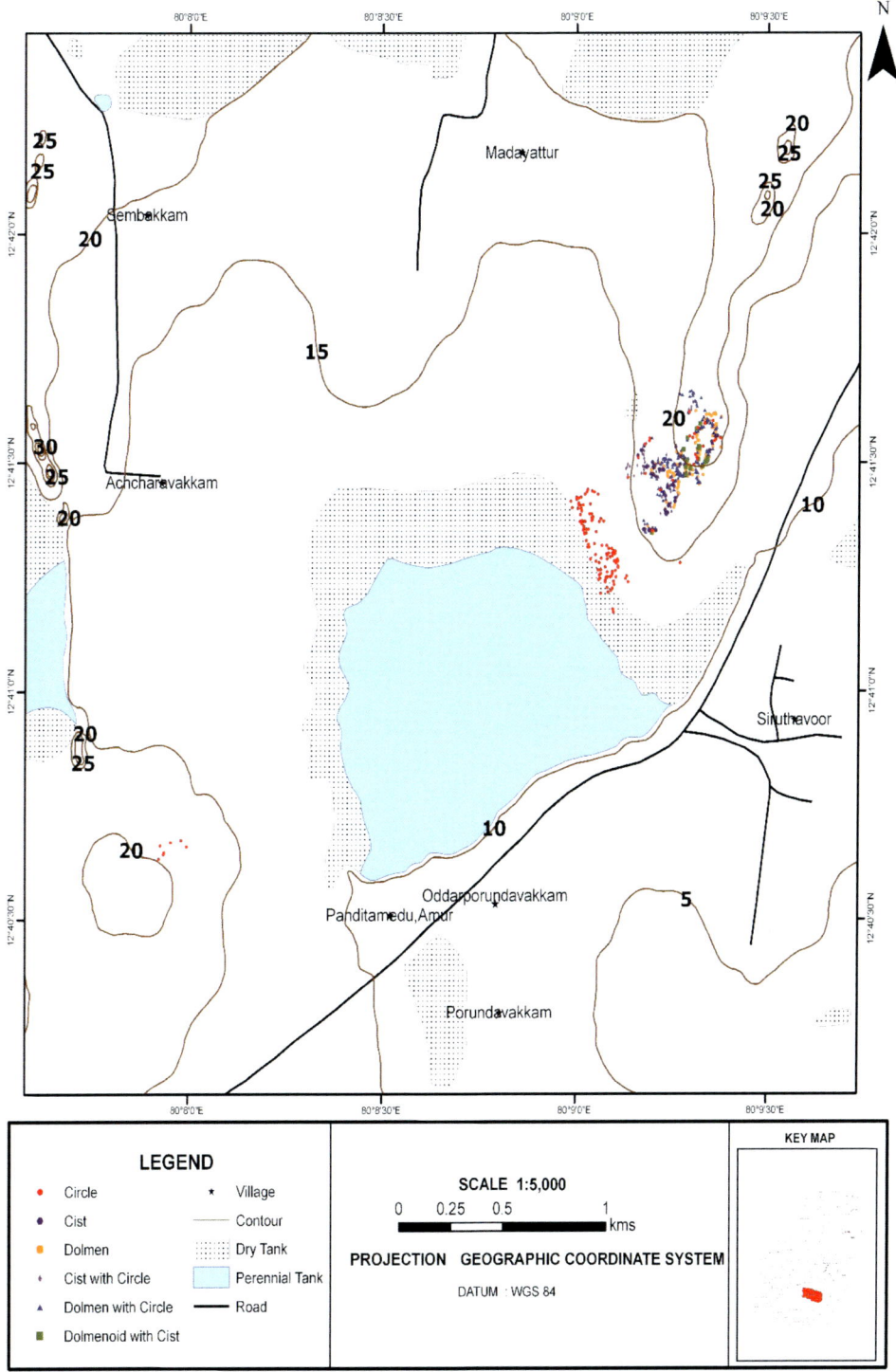

FIGURE 4.12 MAP OF SIRUTHAVOOR SHOWING ALL THE BURIAL TYPES INCLUDING CAIRN CIRCLE, DOLMEN, CIST, DOLMEN WITH CIRCLE, CIST WITH CIRCLE AND DOLMENOID CIST

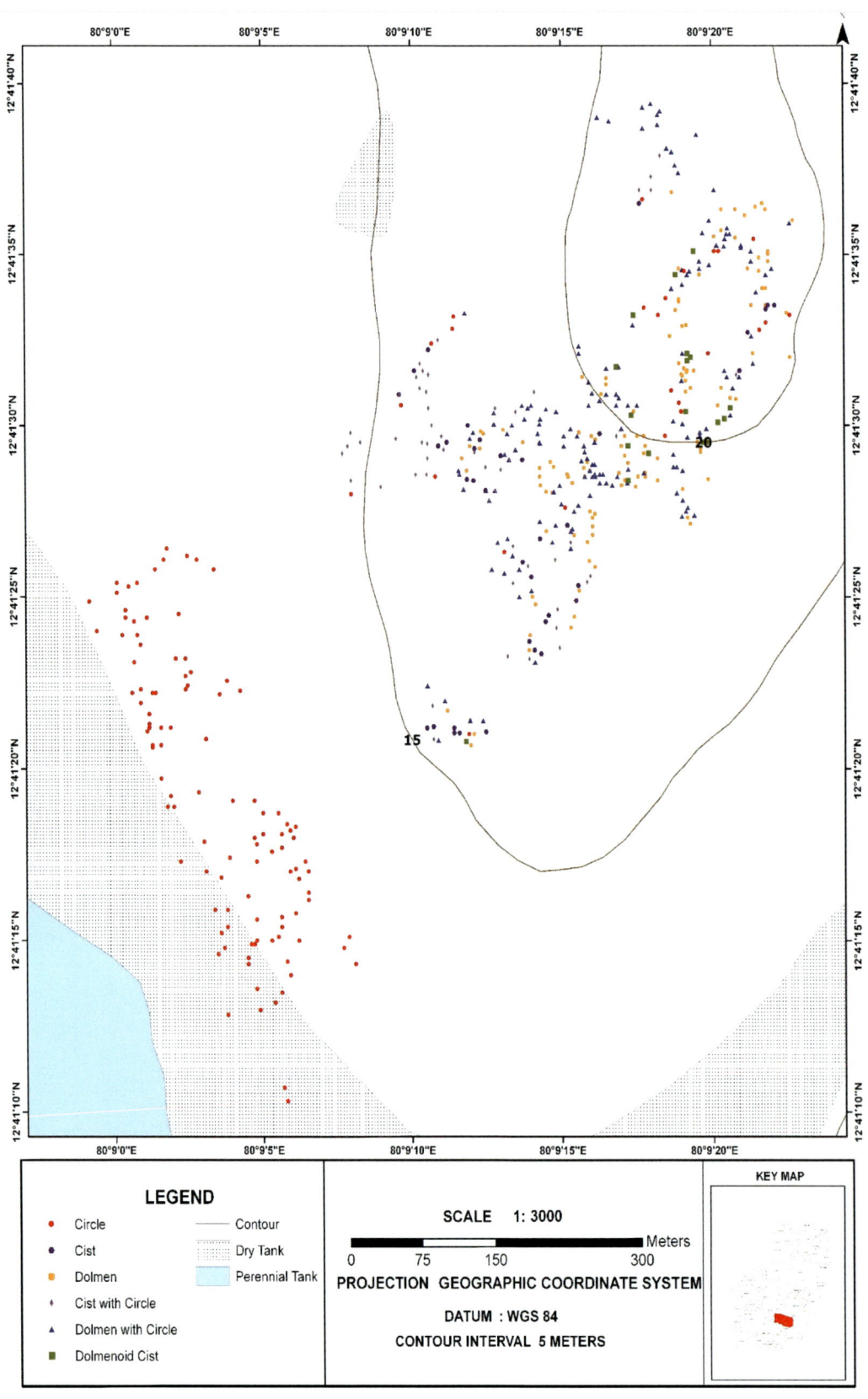

Figure 4.13 Over all map of Siruthavoor (close up) showing the spatial outlay of all IA-EH burials at Siruthavoor

CHAPTER 4 EXPLORATION AND EXCAVATION AT SIRUTHAVOOR

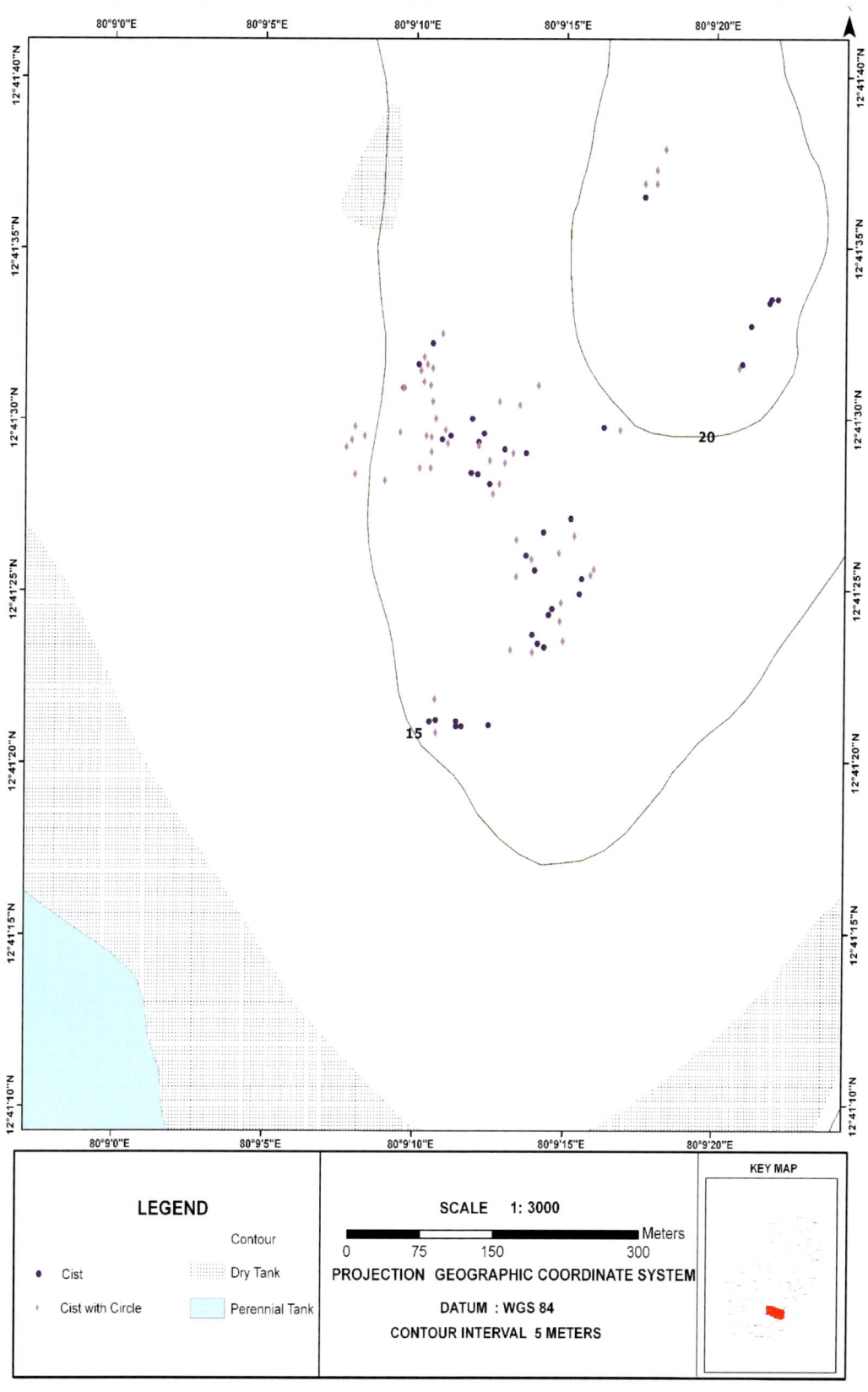

FIGURE 4.14 SPATIAL OUTLAY CIST AND CIST WITH CIRCLE TYPE BURIAL AT SIRUTHAVOOR

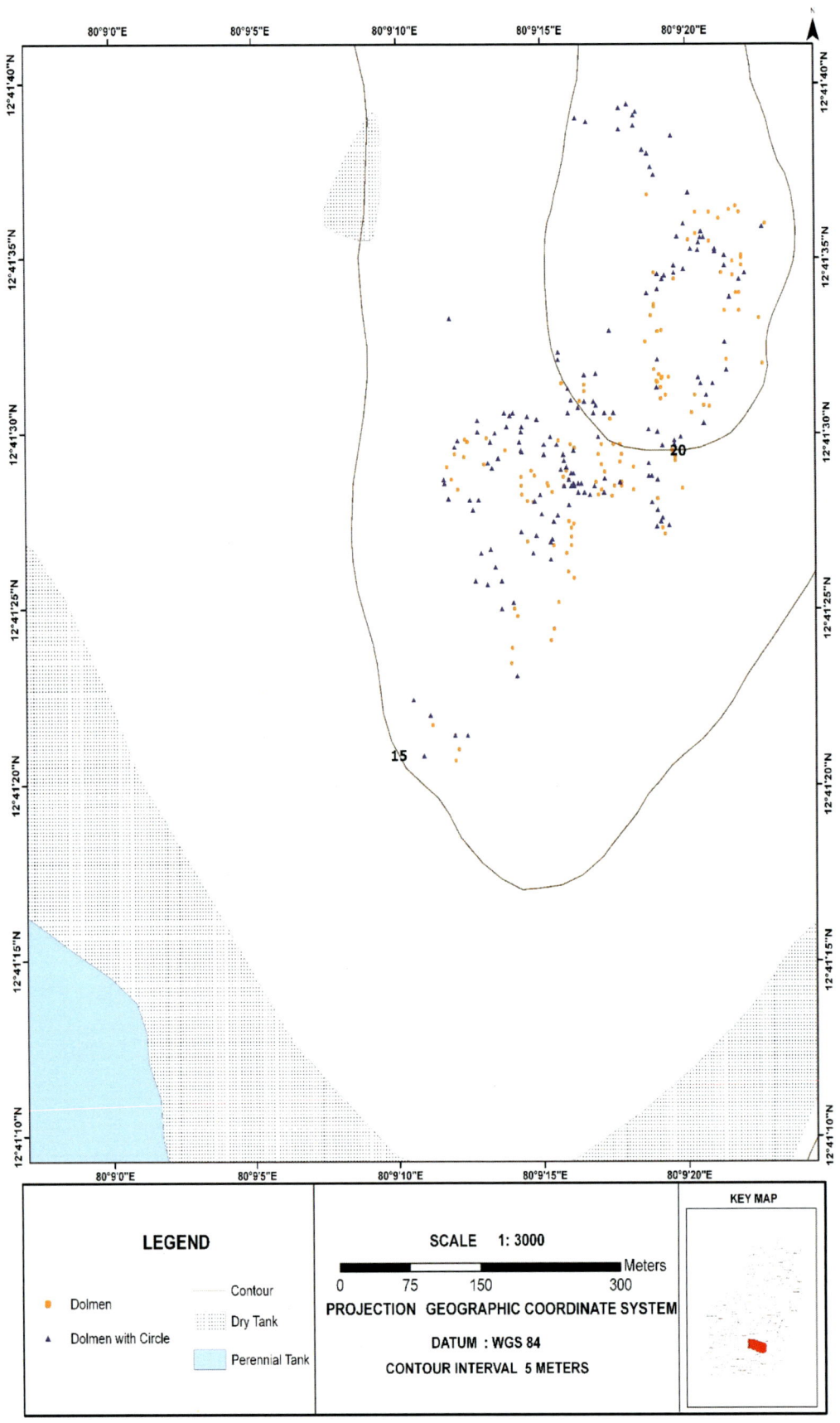

FIGURE 4.15 SPATIAL OUTLAY OF DOLMEN AND DOLMEN WITH CIRCLE TYPE BURIALS AT SIRUTHAVOOR

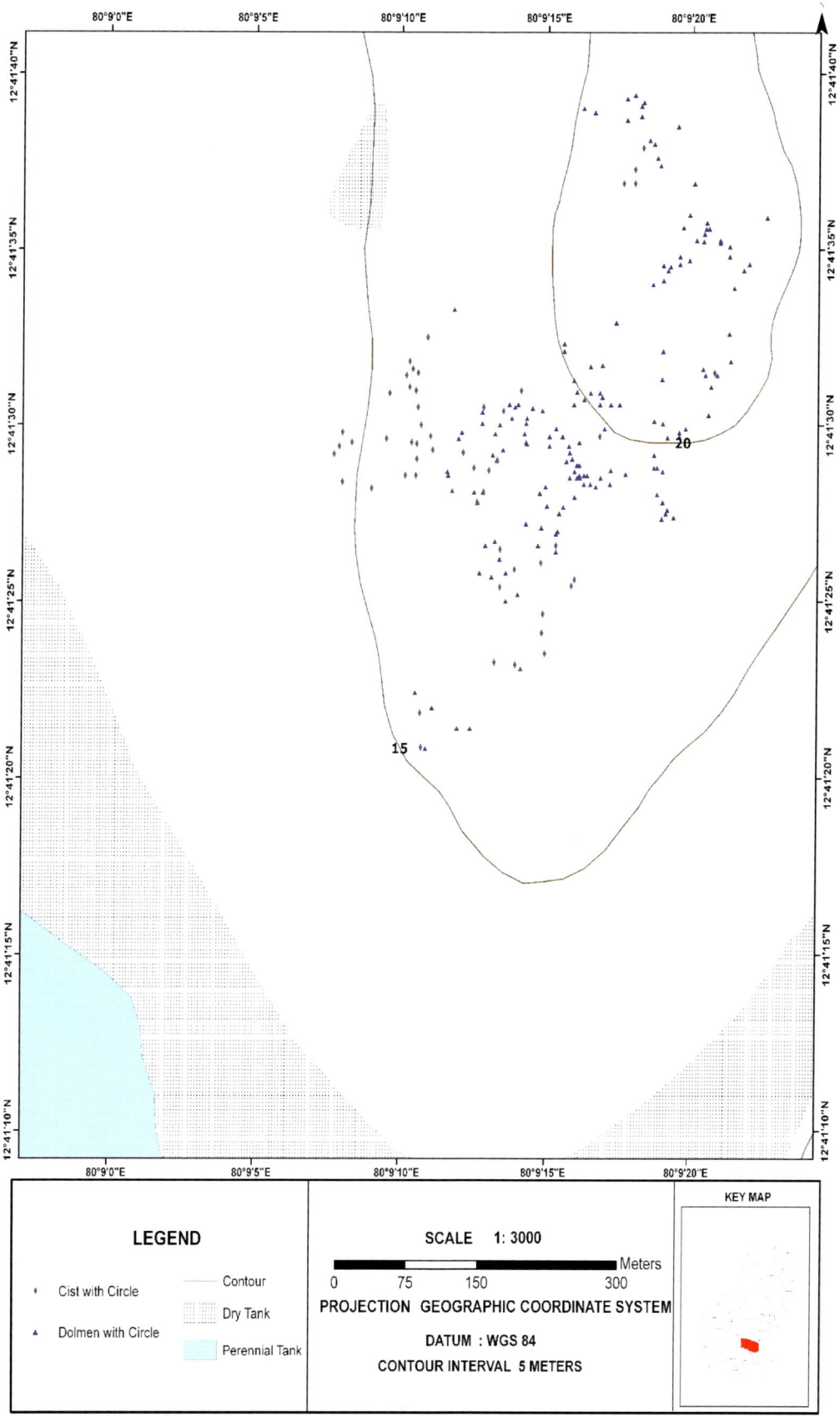

FIGURE 4.16 SPATIAL OUTLAY OF CIST WITH CIRCLE AND DOLMEN WITH CIRCLE TYPE BURIALS AT SIRUTHAVOOR

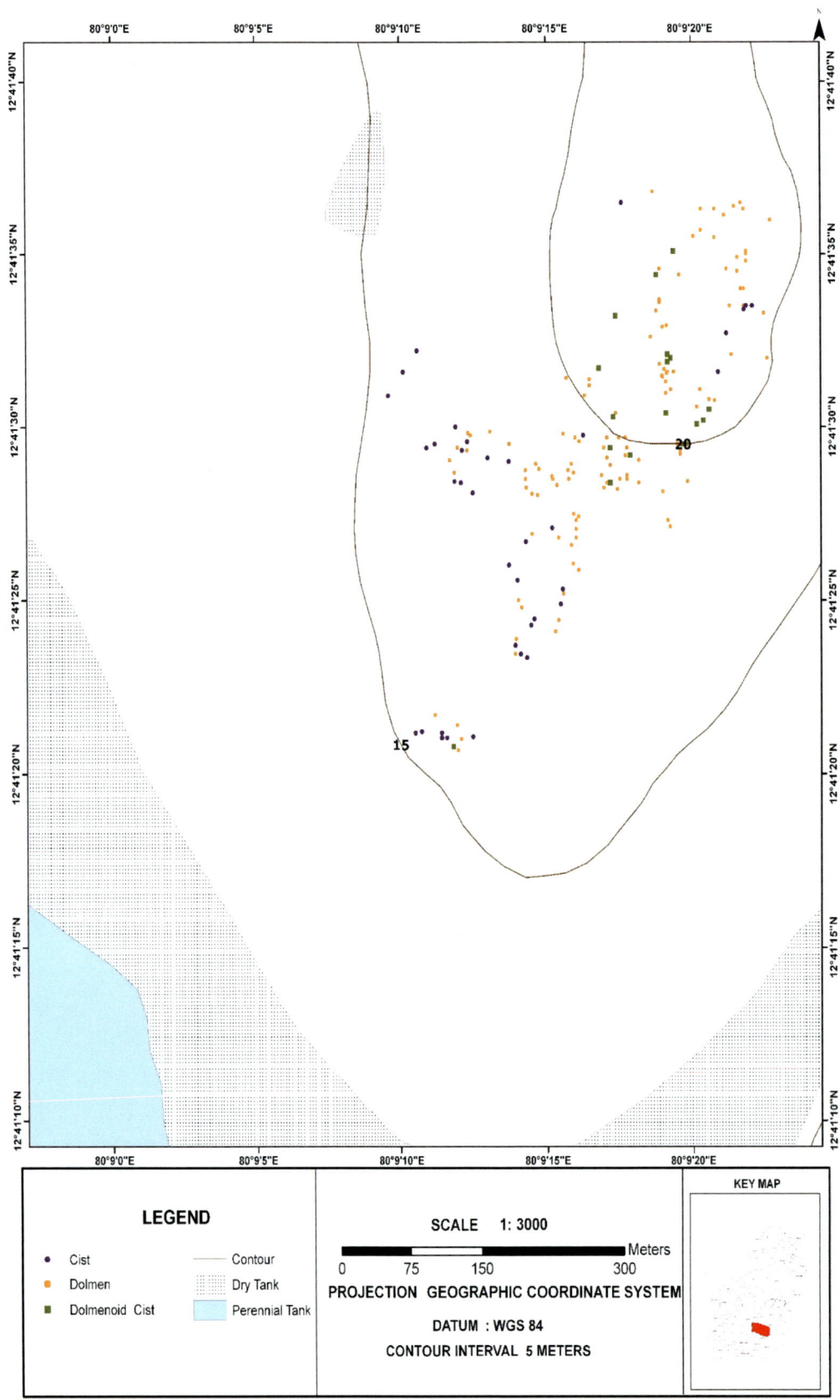

Figure 4.17 Spatial outlay of dolmen, cist and dolmenoid cist type of burials at Siruthavoor

CHAPTER 4 EXPLORATION AND EXCAVATION AT SIRUTHAVOOR

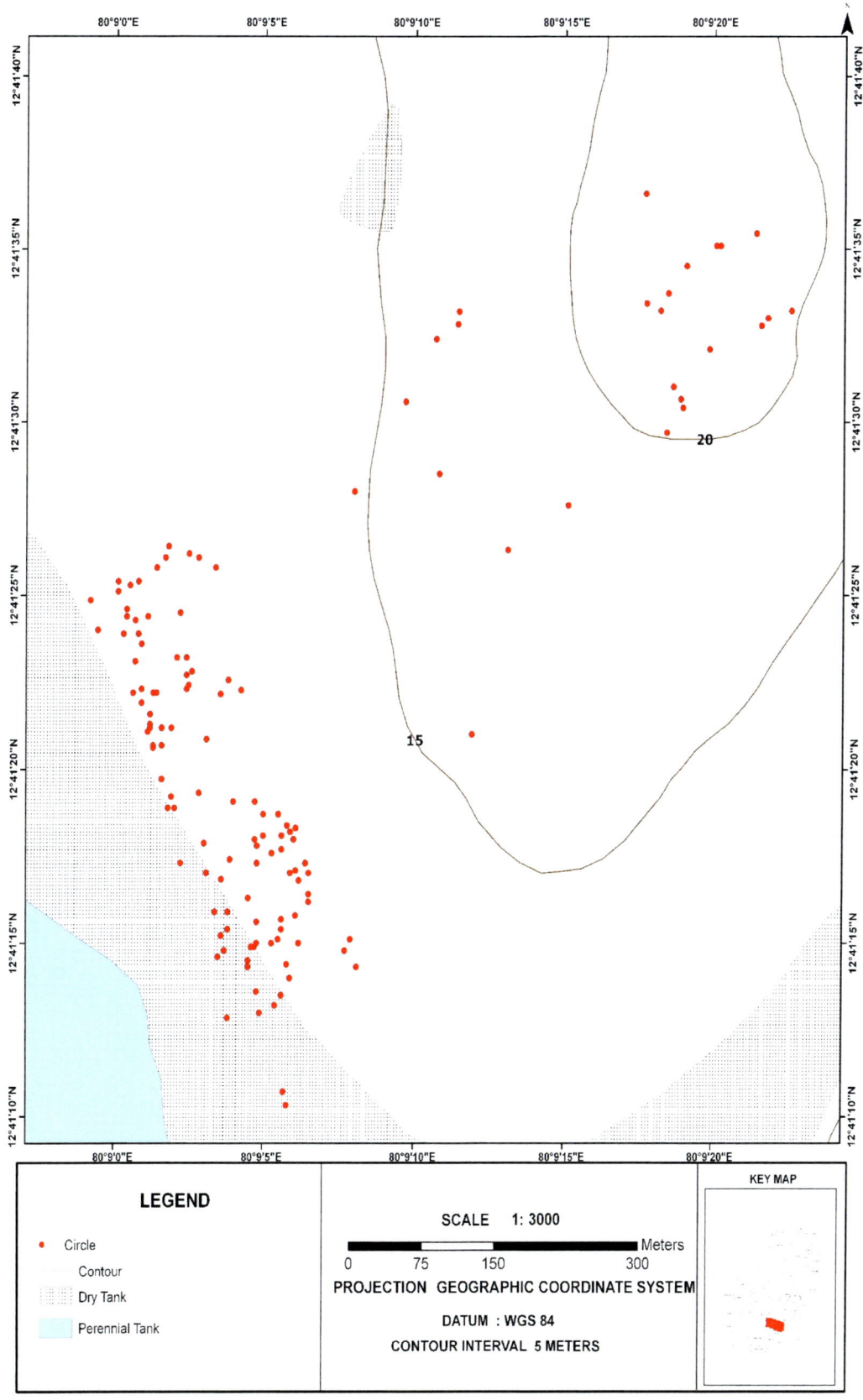

FIGURE 4.18 SPATIAL OUTLAY OF CAIRN CIRCLE TYPE BURIALS AT SIRUTHAVOOR

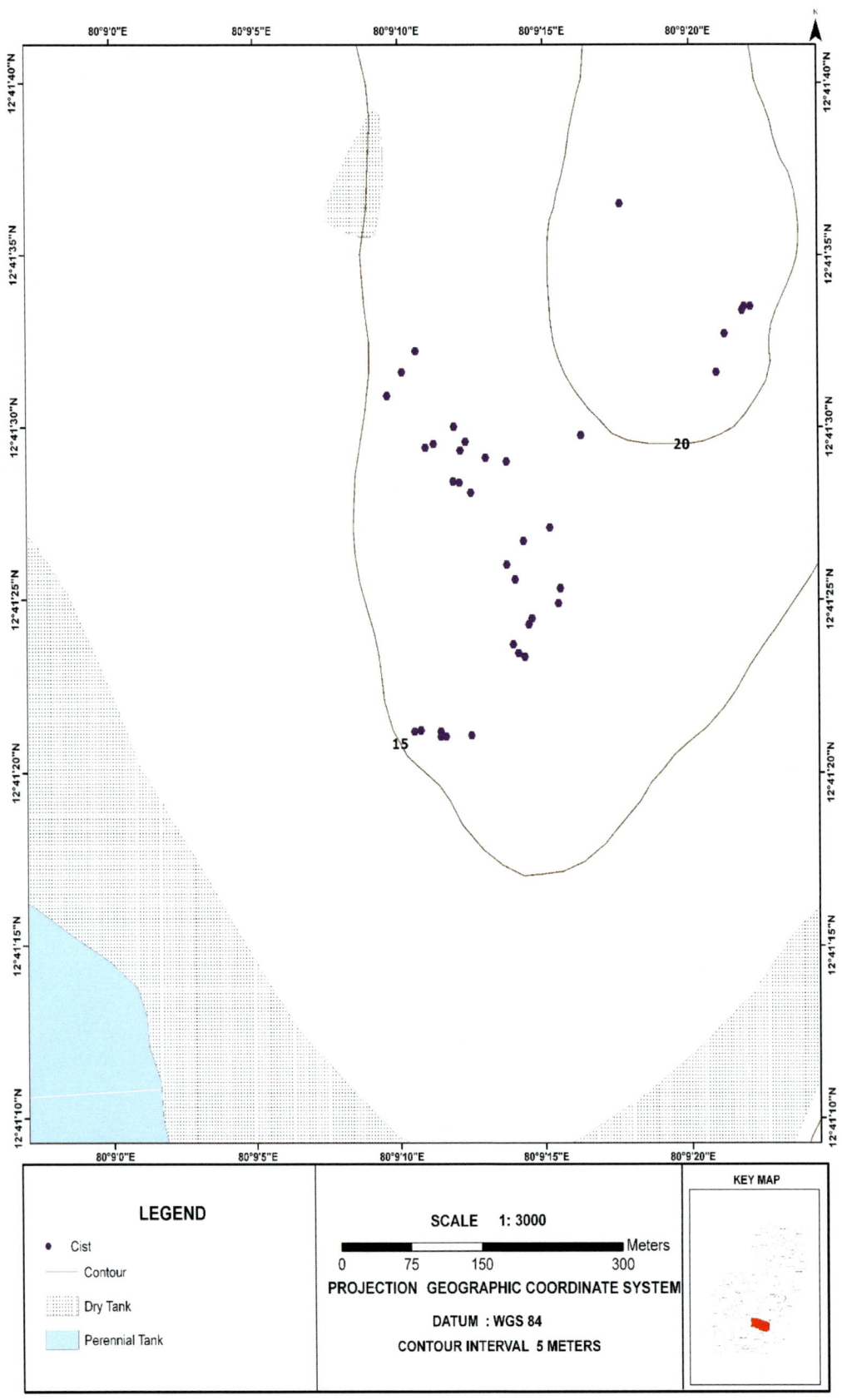

Figure 4.19 Spatial outlay of cist type burials at Siruthavoor

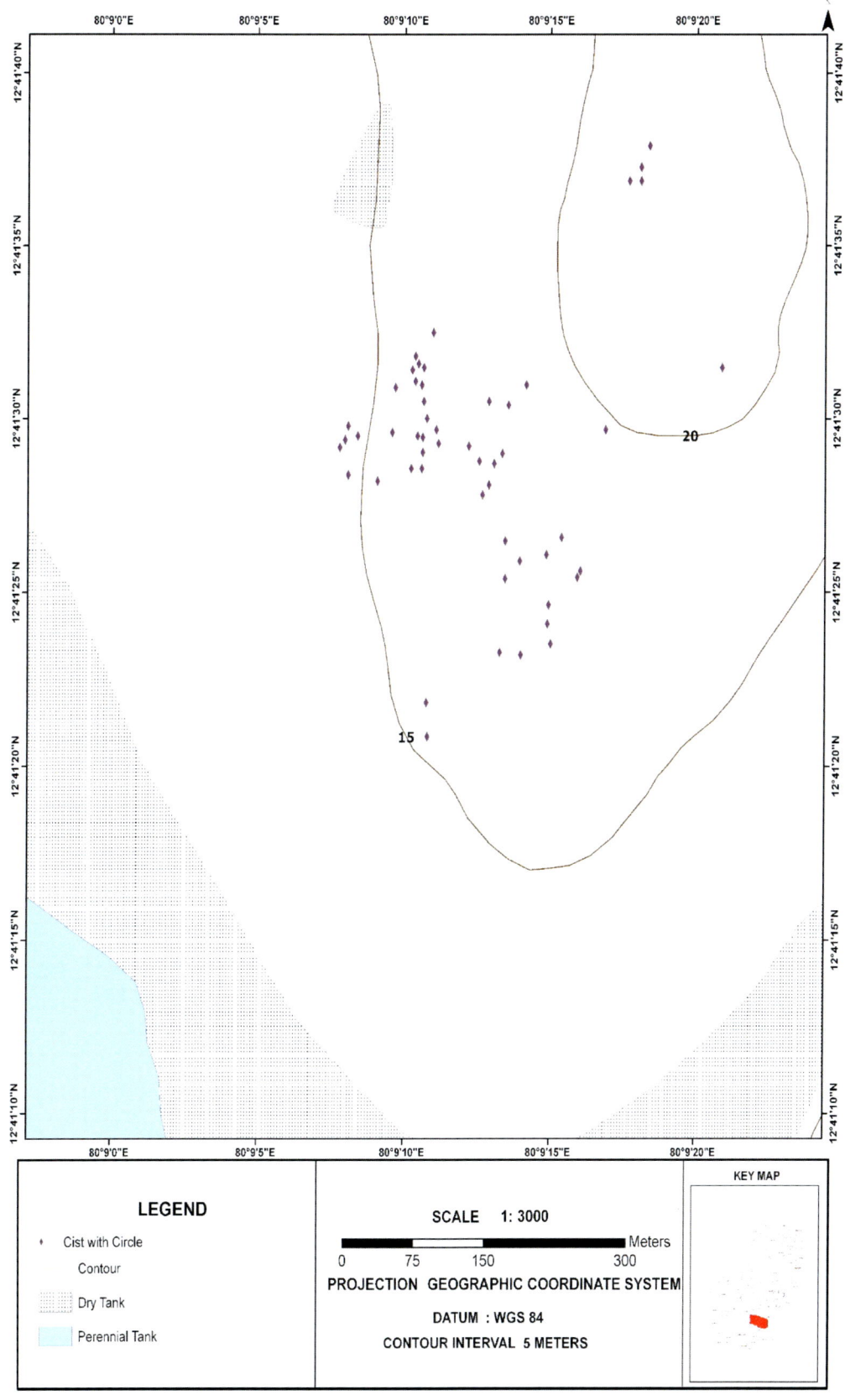

FIGURE 4.20 SPATIAL OUTLAY CIST WITH CIRCLE TYPE BURIALS AT SIRUTHAVOOR

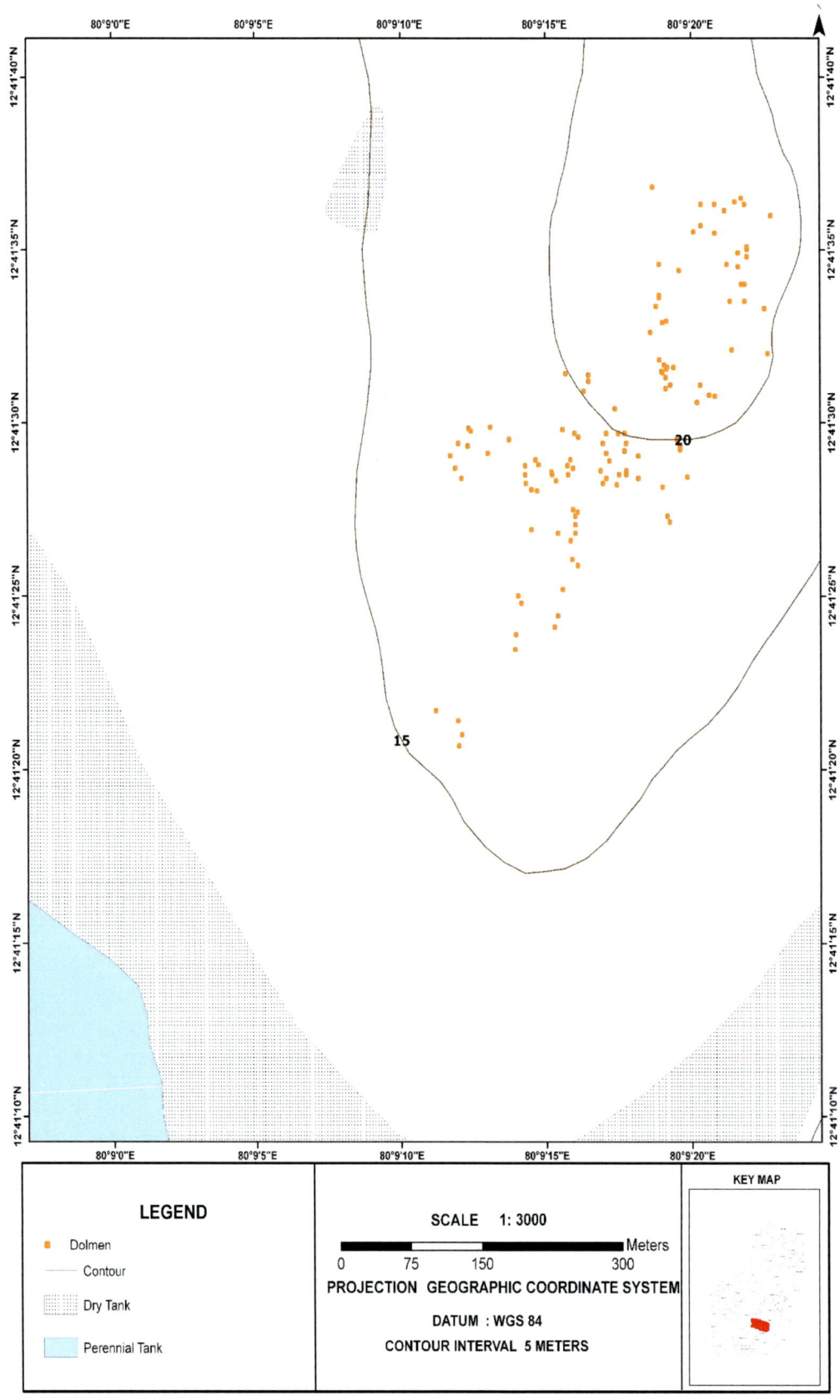

Figure 4.21 Spatial outlay of dolmen with circle type burials at Siruthavoor

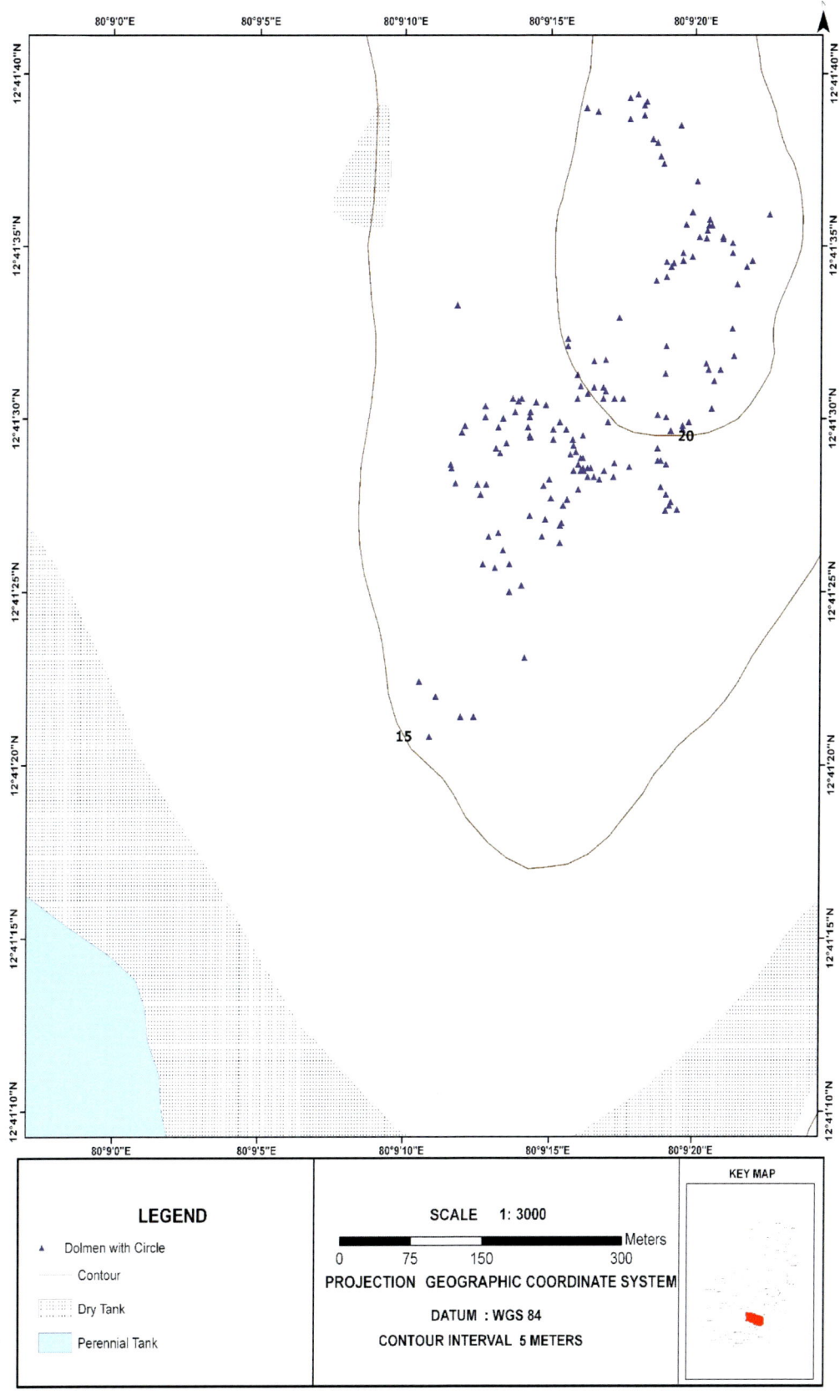

FIGURE 4.22 SPATIAL OUTLAY OF DOLMEN TYPE BURIAL AT SIRUTHAVOOR

4.3.1 Cairn Circle

Around 30% of the Cairn circle situated close to (on the bank of) the Siruthavoor Lake had distinctly visible cairn packing (Figure 4.1). However half of the cairn circles were exposed due to the disturbances caused by water activity with very few having what could be described as a cairn packing visible on the surface. The surface of the Cairn circles, to a large extent had a sandy pinkish white deposit, especially closer to the Lake. Some of the circles also had stone slabs visible inside the circle, but no clear shape was discerned to be able to distinguish them as having either a cist within the circle or a single vertical stone slabs. On an average around 12 stones were found in each circle, with a maximum up to 18 stones. Lateritic blocks and well-rounded boulders were found largely in the eastern or northeast of the Cairn Circle (Figure 4.23), either inside or outside the circle and sometimes also as part of the circle. In some areas the sand quarrying activity was carried out in such way that an island of stones with a nearly intact circle exposed in section was revealed.

FIGURE 4.23 CAIRN CIRCLE WITH LATERITIC BLOCKS OUTSIDE CIRCLE

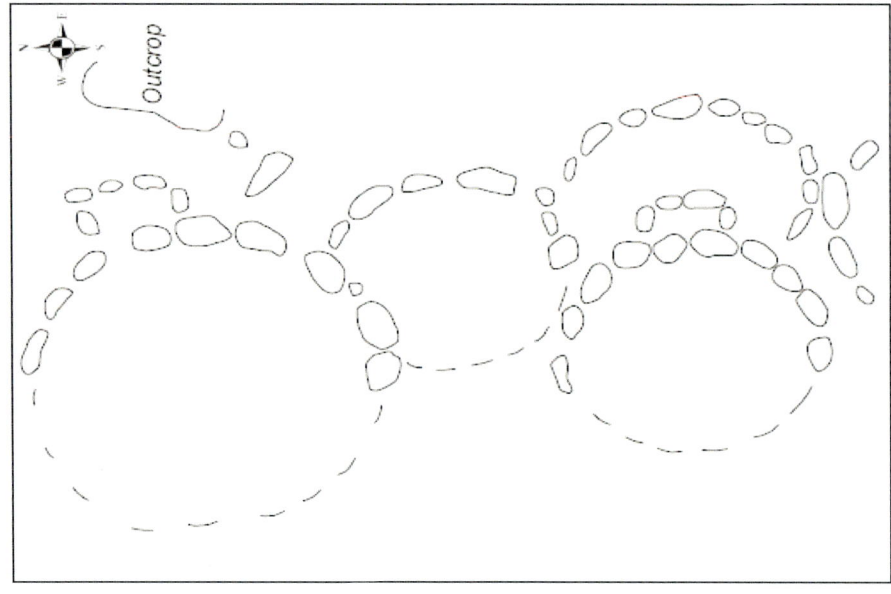

FIGURE 4.24 CAIRN CIRCLE AROUND HILLOCK SHOWING OVERLAP OF BURIALS

CHAPTER 4 EXPLORATION AND EXCAVATION AT SIRUTHAVOOR

Fewer cairn circles were found near the hillock when compared to the number located near the Lake, the former have a distinct cairn packing, much more visible than the ones near the Lake. Towards the northwestern side of the hill, a group of 4 circles were documented as overlapping each other and forming a pattern (Figure 4.24). Two of the circles also had a smaller circle or box like feature attached to the east of the circles.

4.3.2 Dolmen

The dolmen at Siruthavoor are of varying types, sizes and shape. One type is a flush capstone placed close to the ground, but many of them had small slabs separating the large capstone from the ground (Figure 4.25). Another type of dolmen had five boulders supporting a slab or boulder on top (capstone), this dolmen had a cairn circle around it and is shaped like a pentagon rather than rectangular or square (Figure 4.26). Another variation of dolmen found at Siruthavoor had long slabs placed in a north south orientation placed on the ground, with an extra third slab on one side leaning into the dolmen and a triangular stone on the eastern side (Figure 4.27). Similar to this was a type of dolmen made of boulders, with the difference being that the boulders are long and longer than the previous type (Figure 4.28). One or two dolmen had an antechamber in front of the dolmen, clearly distinguishable from those without one (Figure 4.29). The natural outcrops are often incorporated into the construction of the dolmen or the circle around them, these are located near the hillock (Figure 4.29, Figure 4.30) as seen in the excavated burial 4 (Figure 4.).

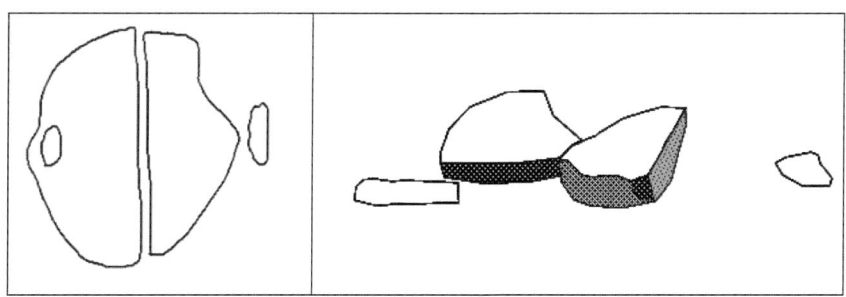

FIGURE 4.25 DOLMEN WITH LOW/FLUSH CAPSTONE

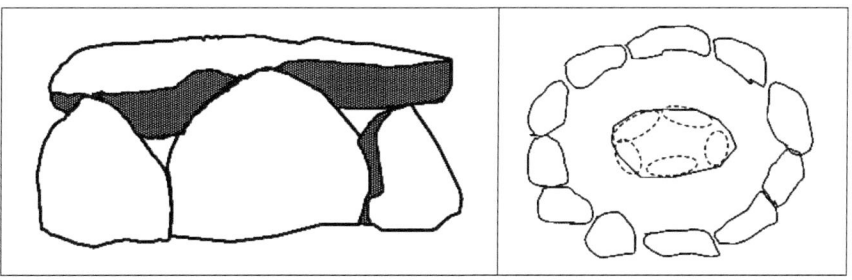

FIGURE 4.26 DOLMEN WITH CIRCLE, DOLMEN HAS FIVE STONES SUPPORTING THE CAPSTONE AND IS CIRCULAR SHAPED

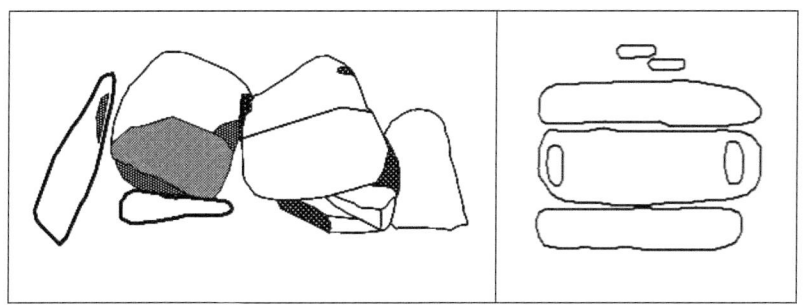

FIGURE 4.27 LOW DOLMEN WITH LONG SLABS AS CAPSTONE

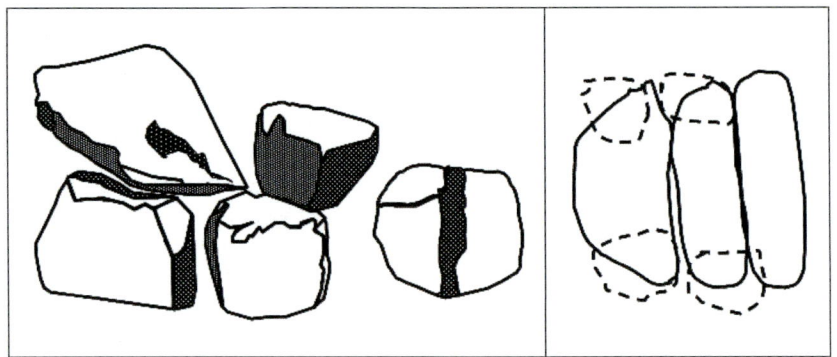

FIGURE 4.28 DOLMEN WITH LONG BOULDER SHAPED STONES

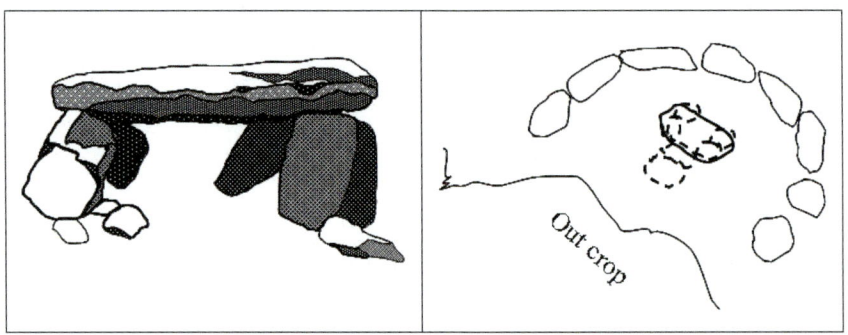

FIGURE 4.29 DOLMEN WITH OUTCROP, AND OPEN ON TWO SIDES

One particular dolmen found to the southern end of the hillock (larger hillock) had a circle around it, the dolmen had a flattened stone placed to the north and a space left between the capstone and this stone created a type of antechamber (Figure 4.30). Towards the northwest of the same dolmen, two boulders were having a flat surface facing the dolmen, rounded at the back and forming a part of the cairn circle.

FIGURE 4.30 DOLMEN WITH SYMBOLIC FEATURES AND OUTCROP USED AS PART OF A DOLMEN

4.3.3 Dolmenoid Cist

Some of the dolmenoid cist burials have rough unhewn stones, and are thicker in breadth, sometimes having a swastika (all references to this word are used to describe the burials with no ritualistic connotations attached to the word) pattern (Figure 4.31 and 4.32). The height of the dolmenoid cist at Siruthavoor is not much, especially when compared to the dolmen. Some dolmenoid cist have no capstone and this may be due to anthropogenic factors, such as stone quarrying currently being carried out by the villagers of Siruthavoor. Due to this reason as well as the unevenness of the terrain and vegetation dolmenoid cists and dolmen are difficult to differentiate from each other clearly.

4.3.4 Cist

Majority of the cists are rectangular, with the occasional square type (Figure 4.33). Some of the cists burials like the circles which are near the Lake have a sandy white deposit. Few of the cists with a circle are not easy to identify due to sediment deposit obscuring the shape of it, and considering that many circles also had slabs within them, care was taken with regards to discerning between the two occurrences of these burial types. The presence of the sandy deposit was noticed as being due to the rise of water level during the rainy season. The height of the cists does not vary a lot but there is a perceptible difference. While the cairn packing is visible for some, others do not have any surface cairn packing and most of them have no visible cap stone. The main types of cist that were observed are the rectangular cists with swastika pattern, the square type which does not have the swastika, and one cist was noticed to be such that, one side cist wall taller than the other three sides (Figure 4.34). Another cist with circle observed near the water body to the northwest of the Siruthavoor Lake, clearly showed a transcepted cist.

Those cists which are exposed in section due to sand quarrying have either urn burial or sarcophagi and sometimes both (Figure 4.35 and 4.36). The sarcophagi have 6 to 15 legs in rows of 2 or 3, and the original shape of both urn and sarcophagi is unclear due to post depositional changes, such as weight of the sediments and stones on them, damage due to plant root and anthropogenic activity. An important aspect noticed during the survey was that, a rectangular pit in the area starting from the Siruthavoor lake running northwest parallel to the hillock (larger) reaching a small water body west of the hillock was affected by sand quarrying activities. However the exposed sections revealed many disturbed or damaged burials, having a slab on top or

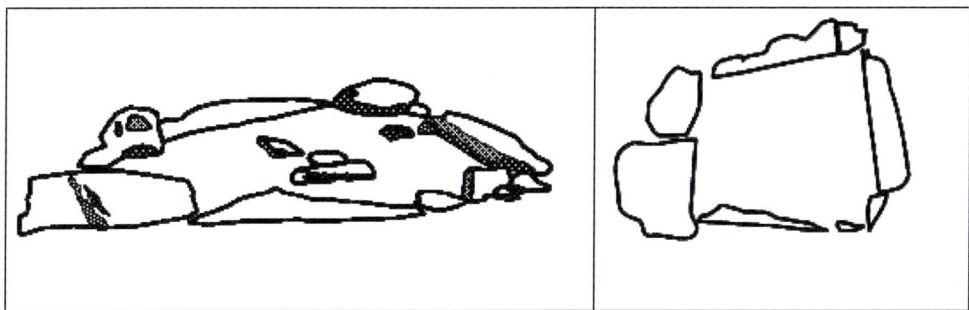

FIGURE 4.31 DOLMENOID CIST SHOWING SWASTIKA PATTERN AND ROUGHLY SHAPED STONES

FIGURE 4.32 DOLMENOID CIST WITH SWASTIKA PATTERN AT AMUR

FIGURE 4.33 CIST BURIAL SITUATED NORTHWEST OF SIRUTHAVOOR LAKE WITH SWASTIKA PATTERN CLEARLY VISIBLE ON THE SURFACE

a swastika shaped cist (Figure 4.36). A large number of sarcophagi were noticed in this area, and a number of iron implements were also noticed during the survey (Figure 4.37). The area north of the Siruthavoor Lake, and south of the hillock was also completely transformed due to sand quarrying, however due to the scale of destruction here even exposed sections were far and few between.

4.3.5 Urn Burials

The urn burials are located close to the water body, which is to the west of the cairn circles, and are exposed due to sand quarrying. They have no stone appendage on the surface, and sometimes have slabs on top of the urn but a few cm below the surface, while others have upturned lids. The size, shape and design on the urns are different to each other.

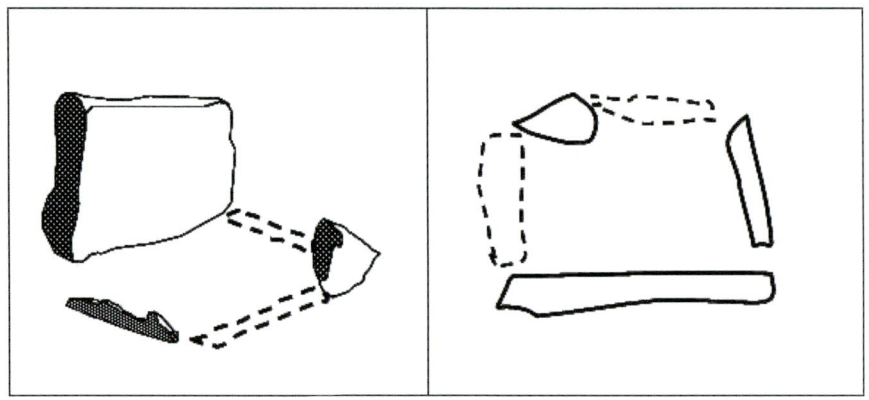

FIGURE 4.34 CIST BURIAL WITH ONE ORTHOSTAT HIGHER ABOVE GROUND THAN REST

FIGURE 4.35 EXPOSED SECTION SHOWING CIST BURIAL

CHAPTER 4 EXPLORATION AND EXCAVATION AT SIRUTHAVOOR

FIGURE 4.36 EXPOSED SECTION OF CIST BURIAL WITH SARCOPHAGUS AND URN SEEN

FIGURE 4.37 IRON IMPLEMENTS FOUND NEAR DISTURBED CIST BURIALS DURING EXPLORATION

4.4 LITHOSECTION

Five sections were litho logged, four of these were without any archaeological material, and the fifth was a composite stratigraphy chosen after studying a number of exposed section with archaeological remains from Siruthavoor (Figure 4.38). All the sections showed a similar weathering profile; with some variation is thickness of sediments. Lithosection 1 was totally 1.23m in height, the lowermost sediment layer seen was 20cm in thickness, with weathering bedrock of gneiss below, with occasional angular cobbles of weathered gneiss and quartz. On top of which was a red (7.5 YR 4/6) coloured strata of 40cm thickness, made up of sediments supported by coarse granular clasts, the clasts being sub rounded to angular, mainly feldsic, with quartz and lateritic pieces. This was followed by a layer of gradational contact of 20 cm thickness, orange (5 YR 7/8) in colour, overlain by matrix supported orange (5 YR 7/6) granular sediments of 20 cm thickness, this layer is normally graded and topped with a surface layer of 23 cm which is pale orange (5 YR 8/4) sandy silt (Figure 4.39 and 4.40).

Lithosecion 2 had a similar weathering profile, with the only changes being in thickness of soil. Litho section 4 however, was a composite stratigraphic section of archaeological stratigraphy, and had a similar base of weathering bedrock material, with angular clasts of gneiss and quartz, red (7.5 YR 4/6) coloured, overlain by a layer of dusky red (7.5 R 4/4) granular clast supported layer, topped by a gradational

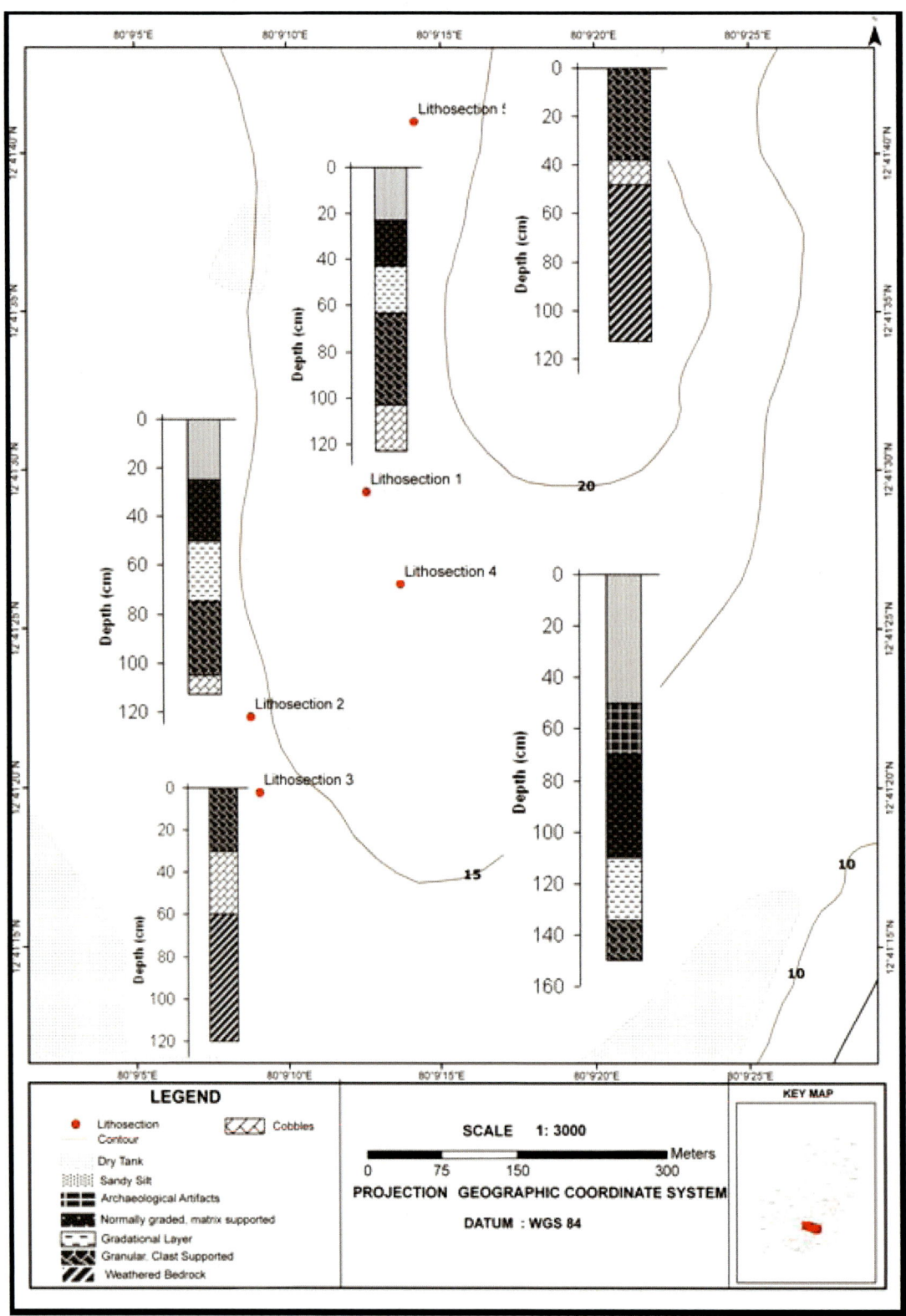

FIGURE 4.38 MAP SHOWING DISTRIBUTION OF LITHOSECTION AT SAIRUTHAVOOR

dull reddish brown (7.5 R 5/3) layer. The archaeological remains which include large slabs of granitic gneiss used in construction of burials and pottery pieces, intrude into a grayish red layer (7.7 R 6/2), pebbly in texture, this is topped by a layer of sandy silt sediments dull orangish red in colour (10 R 6/3). The lithosections 3 and 5 have a thicker layer of bedrock around 60 cm followed by a layer of angular red (7.5 YR 4/6) coloured clasts, overlain by dusky red (7.5 R 4/4) granular sediments. The location of these lithosections shows that the elevated bedrock is seen to be interspersed between the sections with thicker soil profile (Figure 4.39 and 4.40).

Chapter 4 Exploration and Excavation at Siruthavoor

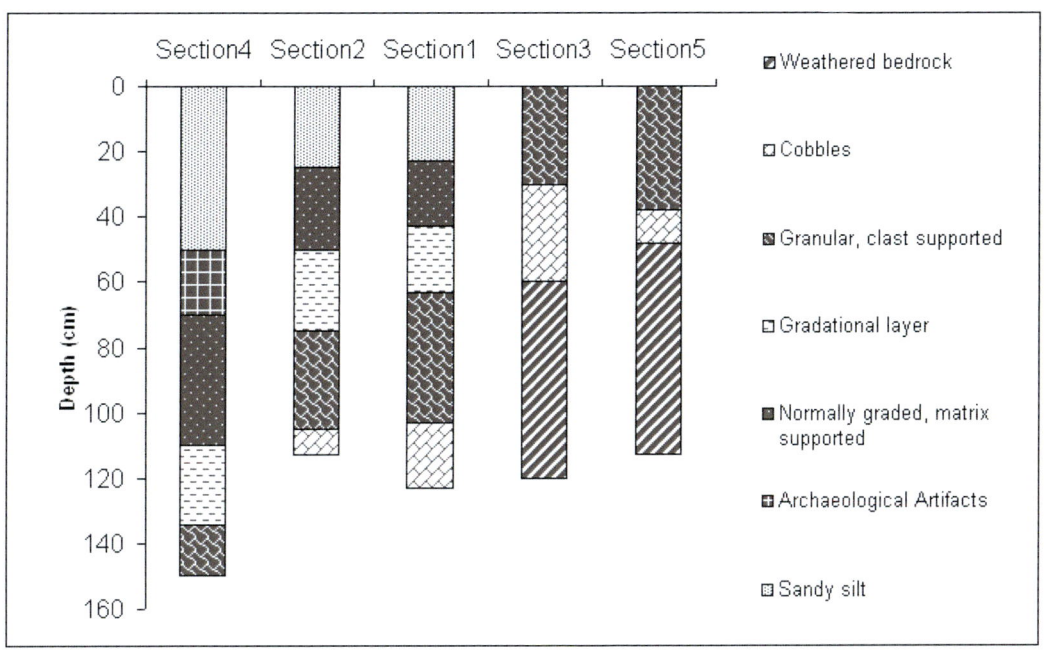

Figure 4.39 Graph of lithosections 1-5

Figure 4.40 Image showing lithosections 1-5 at Siruthavoor

4.5 EXCAVATION

As earlier mentioned eight burials were excavated at Sirthavoor, out of these, Burial 1, 4, 5 and 6 were intact burials, while burials 2, 3, 7 and 8 were partially disturbed/ exposed and burials 2, 7 and 8 did not have any associated stone appendage (Figure 4.41). Burial 3 was the least disturbed, a cist burial, missing half its cairn circle, and the western cist wall was partially intact. However the cist itself was nearly completely preserved. Since the site is being destroyed due to sand quarrying these burials (2, 3, 7 and 8) were excavated with the view of not only getting more information but also salvaging data from already disturbed burials.

Siruthavoor: An Iron Age-Early Historical burial Site, Tamil Nadu, South India

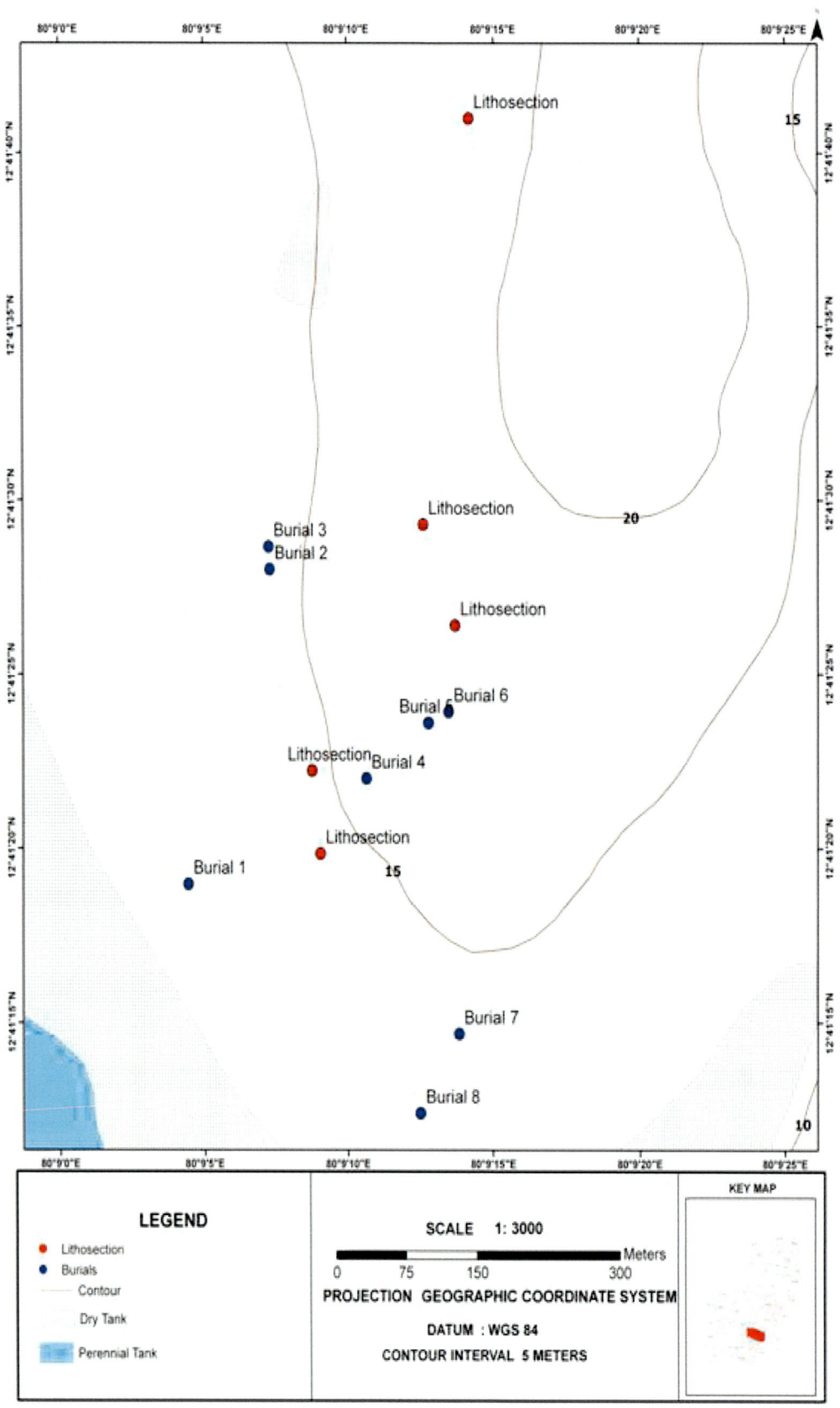

Figure 4.41 Distribution of excavated burials and lithosection at Siruthavoor

4.5.1 Excavation of Burial 1 (Cairn Circle)

Burial 1, a cairn circle, located close to the Siruthavoor Lake was excavated with the aim of understanding construction patterns of burials in Siruthavoor. The surface of the cairn circle was flat, remnants of what may have been cairn packing was noticed in the form of scattered cairn stones within and around the burial. The circle measured 5.90 x 5.10 m on the inside (outer circle measuring 6.33 cm NS and 6.93 EW cm). Inside the cairn circle on the eastern side a rounded stone was located, the rounded side of this stone faced the middle of the circle, its flat side resting upon the cairn circle stone (Figure 4.42). To explore if there was any further evidence of deliberate placement of this extra inner stone in the east and any other associated material; the circle was divided into east and western quadrants and the eastern half was excavated first. Initially a balk of 0.50 m width was kept, dividing the eastern and western quadrants, which was removed after the western quadrant was excavated so as to understand the stratigraphy of both the quadrants.

Four 1x1m trenches were placed outside the circle and were referred to as NE Outer, NW Outer, SW Outer and SE Outer due to their position. These trenches were laid in order to check and verify if any cultural activity was going on outside the circle. While clearing the outer area of the cairn circle, 4 stones were found placed roughly in the four cardinal directions (N,S,E,W) measuring roughly around 12x10x3 cm each underlining the importance of understanding any activities carried outside the circle. Towards the south of the eastern stone inside the circle a pile of laterite pieces were noticed during the excavation. These laterite pieces were completely exposed at depth of 35 cm and on an average they measured 30x15x10cm individually and all together it measured in a cluster 70 x 65 cm. The soil around this feature was much looser, fine and ashy in colour.

At a depth of 33cm the eastern facing section of this burial revealed a pit marking. Four layers were identified from this excavation, the lower or 3rd layer most being the natural soil (Figure 4.43), was a lateritic red coloured soil, very compact and gravelly in texture (10 R 5/8, Red), overlain by the 2nd layer, a mixed brownish sediment of clay mixed with laterite gravel (5 YR 6/3, dull orange), 25 cm in thickness, having some pebbles and this was overlain by a 30 cm deposit of finer brown sediments (5 YR 6/4, dull orange), which was more sandy and less clayey and the 1st layer on the surface. The 4th unit was a clearly demarcated pit which cut into the first 2nd and 3rd layers of the section. Its shape was outlined with angular granitic gneiss. The sediments from the pit were compact, fine in texture, and light reddish grey in colour (2.5 YR 7/1) (Figures 4.42 and 4.43).

FIGURE 4.42 PLAN OF BURIAL 1 AT SIRUTHAVOOR, SITUATED CLOSE TO THE LAKE, HAVING AN EXTRA STONE INSIDE THE CAIRN CIRCLE IN THE EAST

FIGURE 4.43 STATIGRAPHY OF BURIAL 1 EASTERN SECTION

FIGURE 4.44 SOUTHWESTERN QUADRANT WITH COARSE RED WARE POTTERY

At an average depth of 32cm the natural soil appeared in the outer areas of the eastern quadrant (the northernmost and southernmost areas), whereby an area of 1.37 m in the centre of the circle where the brownish layer continued was dug further. This area started from 1.99 m from the northern side towards the centre of the circle and 1.74 m from the southern side to and 1.12 m from the eastern side forming a roughly oval shape. Towards the south east of the granitic gneiss slab was another pit formation which was 35 cm deep covering an area of 3.05X4.35 m, excavation of this pit revealed angular slabs of granitic gneiss and charnockite measuring an average of 36x10x14cm held together with a compact clayey deposit of similar texture and colour as the pit from the section (Figure 4.43). Small pottery pieces were recovered from this pit at depths of 38, 42 and 60cm, they was very weathered but recognizable as Red Ware. This pit ended at a depth of 75 cm below which the lateritic soil was encountered and left undug.

The outer trenches (1x1 m) had two layers, a finer brown sediment (5 YR 6/, dull orange), which was more sandy and less clayey and the 1st layer on the surface of 33cm thick similar to that of the circle. Below this was a 2nd layer of looser lateritic red coloured soil with patches of, very compact and gravelly in texture (10 R 5/8 Red). The 4th layer, namely the pit as well as the intermediate layer numbered 2 in the cairn circle, was missing in the outer trenches. Some fragmentary pieces of coarse and fine Red Ware were recovered in the southwest and southeast outer trenches at a depth of 33 cm and 30 cm respectively (Figure 4.44).

A large slab of gneiss was located at a depth of 50cm in the northeastern quadrant of the trench measuring (25x67x70 cm). When completely exposed the sediments below the slab was seen to be having the same stratigraphic sequence as the east facing section, the complete thickness of soil below this slab being 46 cm, 32 cm of sediments same as 2nd layer and 14 cm of the 3rd layer (Figure 4.43). The position of the slab was such that it sloped from the northern part of the circle towards the centre of the circle.

In the western quadrant at depth of 16 cm, a sarcophagus of 22 cm long was noticed, the sarcophagus oriented in an east west direction, around it was a roughly circular alignment of stones (Figure 4.45). Along with the sarcophagus some broken pottery pieces of fine Ware, in a very badly preserved state were noticed. Iron

Chapter 4 Exploration and Excavation at Siruthavoor

FIGURE 4.45 WESTERN QUADRANT SHOWING SARCOPHAGUS

FIGURE 4.46 BURIAL 1 AFTER EXCAVATION OF EASTERN AND WESTERN QUADRANTS SHOWING STONE ASSEMBLAGE IN THE CENTRE

implements in a very fragile state were also recovered; the shape of the object was not recognizable due to its bad preservation. Some holes were noticed around to the sarcophagus, the body of the sarcophagus had tiny holes but was completely broken. After the balk was removed, it was noticed that long many sided slabs of granitic gneiss were located between the two sides of the circle, or in the centre of the circle. These slabs looked dressed, but did not form any recognizable structure or formation (Figure 4.46).

4.5.2 Excavation of Burial 2 (Sarcophagus)

During preliminary field survey a sarcophagus was partially exposed due to sand quarrying and erosion activity, situated to the northwest of the Siruthavoor Lake. At previous excavated sites such as Sanur and Kunnattur sarcophagi in stone lined pits have been reported (Krishnaswami and Saran 1955, 1956, 1957, Banerjee and Soundara Rajan 1959). This exposed sarcophagus had no stone appendage in its immediate proximity; however presence of disturbed cairn stone's were noticed on the surface around the sarcophagus, but whether it formed a circle or was associated with the sarcophagus was not clear. The objective of excavating this burial, which was disturbed, was to understand if it was buried within any stone appendage or pit.

A 3x 3 m trench was laid encompassing the exposed sarcophagus, but as the burial was very disturbed both stratigraphy and pit markings were difficult to demarcate. The sarcophagus was oriented in a northwest-southeast direction and was exposed at 45 cm (Figure 4.47). The trench did not reveal any associated stone appendage but broken pottery pieces were recovered from the northeastern end of the sarcophagus. The soil in the first layer was mostly loose and bright brown (2.5 YR 5/8) in colour and was 45 cm thick and was redeposited from sand quarrying activity, below this is a 30 cm thick orange (2.5 YR 7/8) coloured sediment.

It was observed that there was a complete lack of stones; the trench was laid on the north-south axis at 1.50 m. the sarcophagus measured 1.65 m in length and 40 cm in breadth and was exposed at a depth 45 cm. The placement of the sarcophagus in the trench was such that it was 1.63 m from the northwestern corner and 2.25 m from the southwestern corner. At the southeastern end of the sarcophagus a possible lid was noticed in broken and fragmentary condition having designs of finger impression all around the upper part and a more elaborate design on the southern facing side of the sarcophagus. The northwestern facing side of the sarcophagus had broken pottery pieces, including Black - and - Red Ware pottery in broken condition due to which the shape was not recognizable. From within the sarcophagus, 13 etched carnelian beads and 3 paste beads (Figure 4.48) were recovered at a depth of 65 cm between the second and third leg of the sarcophagus. The sarcophagus itself was completely exposed at a depth of 95 cm. At the western side of the sarcophagus, a few Black-and-Red Ware pottery pieces (maybe bowl) were noticed and Red Ware pieces in fragmentary condition.

4.5.3 Excavation of Burial 3 (Cist)

Burial 3 was a partially disturbed cist burial with half a circle around it, though one wall of the cist was half uncovered, and some pottery pieces and iron implements were visible. The cist measured 2.47 m (southern orthostat), 1.16 m (eastern orthostat, thickness being 18 cm) 1.46 m (western orthostat, thickness being 15 cm) and inside the eastern wall measured 1.10 m (Figure 4.49). On the inside of the eastern side of the cist an extra slab was present, which sealed the gap between the eastern and southern orthostat. The plan of the cist was that of a swastika, and the slabs used for the orthostat were dressed, and shaped. The sediments in this burial were uniformly red (10 R 5/8) in colour, compact and sandy silt in texture, with very little or no variation.

Two individual arrangements of cairn packing were noticed outside the eastern and southern sides of the cist (Figures 4.50 and 4.51). The stones used in the cairn packing measured an average of (large) 31 x 24 x 17cm and (small) 30 x 31 x

FIGURE 4.47 BURIAL 2: EXPOSED SARCOPHAGUS WITH REMNANTS OF LID

CHAPTER 4 EXPLORATION AND EXCAVATION AT SIRUTHAVOOR

FIGURE 4.48 IRON IMPLEMENTS AND BEADS FROM EXCAVATED BURIALS AT SIRUTHAVOOR

FIGURE 4.49 BURIAL 3: CIST TYPE BURIAL WITH FOURTH ORTHOSTAT DISTURBED

40 cm. These arrangements formed a rectangular path towards the cist without any pebbles or boulders found anywhere else around the cist. At a depths of 28 and 67 cm within the stone packing of the southern side Red Ware pottery were noticed, the pottery from the 28 cm were fine while those at 67 cm were coarse.

An sword like iron implement with a hilt, exposed in the western part of the cist was at depth of 55 cm, a few other smaller iron implements were found at this level (Figure 4.48). At a depth of 63 to 67 cm inside the cist, complete pots along with iron implements was excavated, some of the pots were in an inverted position while others were upright and with sediments found between the different levels (Figure 4.52) . The pots were of varied shapes and while occasionally Black and Red Ware bowls were also noticed a majority of them were Red Ware and rounded bottoms. The base of the sarcophagus was noticed at depth 66 cm while the legs of the sarcophagus were uncovered at

Figure 4.50 Outside cist, cairn packing on eastern and south eastern areas

Figure 4.51 Slab on top of cist with cairn packing on top with slab in eastern side

a depth of 90 cm. The sarcophagus measured 2.10 m x 0.60 m width, however it was too fragmentary to be recovered as a whole and the height of the wall can only be approximated. Around the sarcophagus at the same depth of 90 cm more pottery was found including Black Ware and Red Ware stands. Two large iron implements were found at this level, rectangular in shape, one placed below the sarcophagus and the other leaning on the eastern orthostat (Figures 4.53 and 4.54). Besides other smaller iron implements carnelian beads were also recovered from within the sarcophagus (Figures 4.48 and 4.53).

Small pieces of flat stone were noticed underneath the legs of the sarcophagus in what seems to be an attempt to rectify the difference in height of the legs (Figure 4.56). The southern orthostat was made up of a huge slab, at the centre of which was a rectangular opening measuring 68 cm in width. At the middle of this opening was a triangular shaped feature carved out of the same slab and 53 cm length and appearing to be a port hole (Figure 4.57).

4.5.4 Excavation of Burial 4 (Dolmen)

Burial 4 was a dolmen, situated next to the smaller hillock at Siruthavoor and north of the Siruthavoor Lake. The reasons for the choice of this burial were multifold, first to understand the relationship between the outcrop present to the east and the dolmen. The burials here were 10 cm to 30 cm in depth and the sediments were reddish orange (10 R 6/8) in colour and sandy silt in texture. The exploration revealed many smaller dolmens around this hillock which may have been symbolic; excavating a burial around this hillock was aimed at clarifying this aspect of the site (Figure 4.58). The surface and sub surface features of the IA-EH

FIGURE 4.52 CIST WITH POTTERY

FIGURE 4.53 IRON IMPLEMENTS FROM BURIAL 3, SWORD LIKE OBJECT AND 2 LARGE IRON SLABS FOUND NEAR SARCOPHAGUS INSIDE CIST

A circular trench was laid around the dolmen for a better understanding its relationship to the outcrop present northeast of the dolmen (Figure 4.59). From the eastern quadrant around the circle Red Ware and Black Ware (maybe stand) pottery pieces were recovered at a depth of 10 cm in the northeastern side of the dolmen next to the natural outcrops. Closer to the dolmen also amongst the outcrops at a depth of 43 cm more pottery was found, in a fragmentary condition. At a depth of 10 cm within the dolmen a Black Ware plate and a small iron implement were noticed. To the west of the dolmen at a depth of 53 cm, a sarcophagus was noticed, the sarcophagus was filled with rounded stones and slabs and no other objects was found around.

4.5.5 Excavation of Burial 5 (Dolmen with circle)

Burial 5 was a dolmen with a circle around it; consisting of five boulders at the base which carried the weight of the capstone which was placed on top of these boulders. While normally dolmen type burials are believed to have a rectangular or square base, the five base stones of this dolmen formed a rough pentagon rather than a box. On the eastern side, was a gap between two of the base boulders and just outside the circumference of which were present two triangular shaped stones. This type of dolmen was also noticed during the field survey, and due to their repeated occurrence on the site understanding these dolmen was important for the further understanding of the typological differences of burials at Siruthavoor.

FIGURE 4.54 SARCOPHAGUS, LARGE IRON IMPLEMENTS AND RED WARE STAND

burials in general differ from one burial to another and excavating this dolmen was important for understanding these differences at Siruthavoor.

FIGURE 4.56 SARCOPHAGUS OF CIST WITH STONE BELOW LEGS TO BALANCE THE STRUCTURE

CHAPTER 4 EXPLORATION AND EXCAVATION AT SIRUTHAVOOR

FIGURE 4.57 SARCOPHAGUS FROM CIST WITH ASSOCIATED GRAVE GOODS

FIGURE 4.58 BURIAL 4: DOLMEN ASSOCIATED WITH OUTCROP, NEXT TO SMALLER HILLOCK

FIGURE 4.59 BURIAL 4 SHOWING ASSOCIATION WITH OUTCROP

FIGURE 4.60 BURIAL 5: DOLMEN IN PENTAGON/CIRCULAR SHAPE WITH TWO TRIANGULAR STONES IN THE EAST

FIGURE 4.61 BURIAL 5 WITH STONE PACKING BETWEEN BOULDERS BELOW CAPTSONE

The soil within the cairn circle, outside the dolmen was orange (2.5YR 7/6), lateritised and hard, mixed with weathered stones. These pebble sized stones also occurred outside the cairn circle, forming part of a cairn packing, but the stones were scattered, evenly distributed within the sediments. The cairn packing was excavated leaving a balk of 50 cm in all four directions. The cairn packing was 40 cm thick, after which the soil texture changed and was left un-dug, in the southeastern quadrant. A stone packing of larger stones, compact in structure and in a rectangular pattern abutted the eastern balk. In the northeastern quadrant Red Ware pottery pieces were found both near one of the cairn circle stones and directly outside the dolmen partly within the eastern balk. The excavation of the circle outside the dolmen also revealed that between the 5 boulders that made up the dolman stone packing made of smaller pebbles and ceiling the gaps between the boulders was revealed (Figure 4.61).

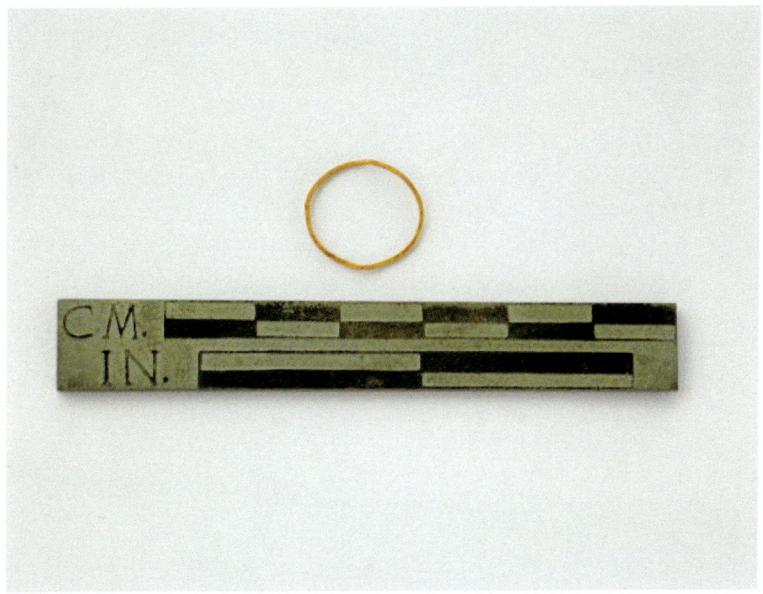

FIGURE 4.62 GOLD RING FROM BURIAL 5

The soil within the dolmen was reddish orange (10 R 6/8) in colour, loosely packed and fine textured, without any distinct variations. Three sarcophagi were excavated within the dolmen and labeled sarcophagus A,B and C. At a depth of 40 cm 2 iron pieces in the western area of the dolmen and on top of sarcophagus A was revealed, a circular arrangement of rounded stones was also exposed roughly placed on top of this sarcophagus (Figure 4.60). Occasional pieces of broken pottery were uncovered within the western part of dolman however the eastern part was completely devoid of any artifacts. While sieving sand from the southwestern area (around western end of sarcophagus A) a gold ring was discovered at a depth of 54 cm (Figure 4.62). It was small in circumference and thin, however the colour was a bright yellow, with no sign of any tarnishing. At the same depth of 54 cm the second sarcophagus, labelled B was exposed in the northeastern area of the dolmen (Figure 4.63).

Two iron implements were discovered, the larger one in the northeast next to sarcophagus A and smaller one in the southwest near sarcophagus B which was partially exposed. At the same depth in the southern part of the dolmen a small translucent white quartzite piece of stone was recovered, apart from this and the stones used for the semi circle on top of sarcophagus A the sediment had no large clasts. Sarcophagus C, which was smaller in length was located in the northeastern most corner of the dolmen. Two of the sarcophagi had designs on their body, while sarcophagus A had a rope like design throughout the upper half of the body, B had a fingerprint design and all three had lids, though disturbed and broken and all the sarcophagi were placed in the east-west orientation. In the western part of the dolmen near sarcophagus A was found a three legged pot at a depth of 60 cm however it was broken and not recovered intact. Sarcophagus A had three rows of legs, 15 in number, while sarcophagi B and C have two rows numbering 12 and 4 respectively. At a depth of 74 cm the natural outcrop on which the sarcophagi were placed was exposed (Figure 4.64).

4.5.6 Excavation of Burial 6 (Dolmenoid Cist)

Burial 6 was a dolmenoid cist burial having no cairn circle around; the cist did not have a capstone. The orthostat of the cist were made of stones which were roughly dressed into slab like forms; they were neither like the boulders used in Burial 4 nor were they dressed slabs like those of Burial 3 (Figure 4.65). The sediments within this burial was very compact with only one unit, this was orange (5

Figure 4.63 Sarcophagi A, B and C within burial 5 with remains of lid on top

Chapter 4 Exploration and Excavation at Siruthavoor

Figure 4.64 Bedrocks on which sarcophagi were kept in burial 5

YR 6/6) in colour and gravely in texture with some pebbles and no variation was sediments was noticed. At a depth of 35 cm pottery pieces (mostly course Red Ware pottery) were recovered, however the pottery excavated form this burial was very weathered, making it impossible to record any shapes. At the same depth as the Red Ware pottery, a possible sarcophagus was excavated on the south east side of the dolmenoid cist. This sarcophagus was placed in an east west oriented and a few pieces were fragmentary Black and Red Ware pottery was recorded on the northeast side. In the northern area of the quadrant at the same depth, a conglomerate of pottery pieces cemented together by sediments was exposed. Further excavation of these revealed two circular impressions which were probably remnants of a pot, the pottery pieces themselves were highly weathered and dark orange in colour, though due to their poor state of preservation the Ware and type were not identifiable.

4.5.7 Excavation of Burial 7 (Urn with Capstone)

Burial 7 is an urn type of burial partly exposed due to human activity. The urn on excavation was found to be intact and had a cap stone measuring 73 cm in width and 9 cm thickness and placed 8 cm above the urn (Figure 4.68). The urn was excavated with the intention of understanding its associated finds and any visible pit markings. No stone appendage was visible on the surface in this area of the site, only due to the large scale anthropogenic activities were the urns exposed and subsequently many of them had been destroyed. No grave goods were found around Burial 7, the urn was 42 cm in width and 33 cm in height with the neck measuring 6 cm. The capstone emerged 22 cm below the surface, this soil was reddish orange (10R 6/8) in colour and hard and compact with a sandy texture. The soil around the urn was red coloured (7.5R 4/8), latertic and very compact and gravely in texture. The urn was covered by a lid, which was broken but clearly visible around the mouth of the urn, inside the urn the soil was fine textured, red in colour (7.5R 4/8) and loosely packed. At the bottom of the urn, a Black and Red Ware bowl with ash and fragmentary bone pieces was recovered, the ash and bone pieces were also found inside the urn around the bowl.

Figure 4.65 Dolmenoid cist type burial, burial 6

FIGURE 4.68 BURIAL 7, URN WITH CAPSTONE

FIGURE 4.69 URN WITH INVERTED LID ON TOP BURIAL 8

4.5.8 Excavation of Burial 8 (Urn)

Burial 8 was exposed along with many other such urns when a ditch had been dug by the Siruthavoor village authorities as drainage for a road which was being laid to the northeast of Siruthavoor Lake. Burial 8 did not have any cap stone or any other associated stone appendage (Figure 4.69). The 1st layer was 31 cm in thickness, and was dump resulting from the road laying activities below this was a lateritic soil not very compact and this layer continued below the urn, the section did not clearly show any pit marking or change in texture. The urn was 71 cm wide at the shoulder, 58 cm at the base and 1.41m height. The trench was 1.50 m in width, with the urn located 39 cm away from the northern wall of the trench.

On the southern section another disturbed urn, was exposed, however this was not further excavated. The excavation of Burial 8 revealed a single urn with an upturned lid on top; very few fragmentary pieces of pottery were recovered from around the urn. The inside of the urn had yellowish soil; the urn was found tilting towards the southwest. The urn also had some clasts of quartzite and gneiss which appeared very weathered. No grave goods or bones were recovered except for a few fragmentary broken pieces of pottery form outside the urn. The output from the survey and excavation carried out at Siruthavoor addresses a few important questions which have often been asked but so far have not been analysed in detail.

The exploration of the sites around Siruthavoor show that other IA-EH burial sites existed within close proximity clearly indicating a landscape in which the people did not live in isolation. On the contrary the proximity of other sites likes Thiruporur and Manamai to Siruthavoor indicates a well populated IA-EH landscape in this region. The burials at Siruthavoor show variations in density of types of burials in specific regions of the sites landscape. The area occupied by the different types of burials are however not completely exclusive of each other, rather they overlap, showing us that chronology, topography as well as social factors could potentially explain this spatial segregation. The previously given classifications (Krishnaswami 1949, Sundara 1979, Moorti 1994, Rajan et al 2009) does not make allowance for all the variations of burial types within a site, nor does it help understand the peculiarities of the types within a site. Rather than try and fit burials into pre existing classification, understanding the burials in terms of chronology and construction methods could prove more effective in collecting more information and data on the IA-EH burials.

The excavation has shown that the different types of IA-EH burials have been placed with topographical context; however survey reveals that this is not the only factor influencing the placement of burial. Excavation reveals that burial 4 and 5 are placed on top of the bedrock, and the outcrop east of burial 4 has integrated into the burial space. However dolmen seen in exposed sections how that they are not all placed only on the bed rock. Excavation has also revealed that the cist burials had a richer variety of grave goods when compared to the other types of burial at Siruthavoor.

Chapter 5
Results

5.1 LABORATORY ANALYSIS OF SEDIMENTS AND POTTERY FROM SIRUTHAVOOR

This chapter details the results obtained from analyzing the sediment samples collected during the excavation and those from one of the litho sections described in the previous chapter. Integration of geochemical and textural data was important in supplementing the field survey, excavation and mapping of the site. The geochemical data can help in identifying the source of sediments and hold signatures for understanding the geological and geomorphological processes operating at the site (Rapp and Hill 2006). The analysis includes textural analyses from sieving and statistical analysis of this data as well as geochemical analysis. The sediment samples were analysed for all major elements, Al_2O_3, SiO_2, NaO_2, K_2O, FeO, MgO, CaO, MnO as well as some trace elements such as Co, Cr, Ni, Cu, Zn and Pb. The sediments were analysed in order to identify the source of the sediments within the burial, as well as investigating whether any drastic erosion or depositional processes which may have altered the surface appearance of these burials. Pottery samples were dated through OSL method in order to obtain a chronology for the burials with specific attention to the type of burial. Besides this the pot sherds from the excavated burials and clay samples from nearby sources as well as a potter in Chennai were analysed for REE to understand their provenance.

5.2 TEXTURAL ANALYSIS

Sediment samples from each burial was collected during the excavation and the sand silt clay ration of the samples has been represented below in tabular and graphical formats. All the sediment samples from the burial as well as the lithosection show a negative correlation between the sand and the silt. For samples where the percentage of sand is high the silt is correspondingly lesser. with very little impact on the percentage of clay. The lithosection shows a high percentage of silt below 80 cm (19.33%, 21.4%) while it reduces above 80cm, except for the 0-20 cm which can be explained as recent anthropogenic activity (Tables 5.1 to 5.5).

5.2.1 Trilinear Diagram of Sand, Silt and Clay Percentages

The sediments from the exposed lithosection 1 at Siruthavoor fall within the sand and loamy sand in nature, while those from all the burials fall within the loamy sand-sandy loam area of the trilinear diagram, indicating an increase in reworking of sediments of the burials (Figures 5.1 to 5.5).

5.2.2 Sieve Analyses

The sieving of the sediments show that amongst the burial sediments except for Burials 2 and 3 all the other burial sediments are largely platykurtic in nature. The sediments of the lithosection alternate between leptokurtic and platykurtic. The lithosection also exhibits dominantly medium and coarse sand, while the burial sediments tend more towards medium and fine sand except for burial 1 (Tables 5.1to 5.10). The data from the lithosection sediments also indicate that below 80 cm the sediments are platykurtic in nature, while above which they are largely leptokurtic.

Depth	Sand	Clay	Silt
10cm	70.78	0.38	28.74
38cm	63.58	0.47	35.95
60cm	63.68	0.29	36.02

TABLE 5.1 TEXTURAL ANALYSIS OF BURIAL 1

Depth	Sand	Clay	Silt
22cm	62.73	0.24	37.02
45cm	69.99	0.23	29.76
65cm	87.89	0.16	11.93

TABLE 5.2 TEXTURAL ANALYSIS OF BURIAL 2

Depth	Sand	Clay	Silt
60cm	64.5	0.22	35.27
67cm	54.08	0.5	45.4
70cm	67.21	0.36	32.42
90cm	62.89	0.46	36.64

TABLE 5.3 TEXTURAL ANALYSIS OF BURIAL 3

Burial	Depth	Sand	Clay	Silt
Burial 4	30cm	70.05	0.36	29.57
Burial 5	35cm	68.96	0.25	30.78
Burial 7	54cm	66.75	0.26	32.97
Burial 7	70cm	62.42	0.15	37.41
Burial 8	50cm	58.39	0.49	41.11

TABLE 5.4 TEXTURAL ANALYSIS OF BURIALS 4, 5, 7 AND 8

Description	Depth	Sand	Clay	Silt
Section 1	0-20	82.37	0.2	17.42
Section 1	20-40	90.35	0.1	9.54
Section 1	40-60	87.89	0.3	11.8
Section 1	60-70	95.15	0.14	4.7
Section 1	70-80	88.51	0.11	11.37
Section 1	80-100	80.66	0.14	19.18
Section 1	100-120	80.42	0.24	19.33
Section 1	120-123	78.45	0.14	21.4

TABLE 5.5 TEXTURAL ANALYSIS OF LITHOSECTION 1

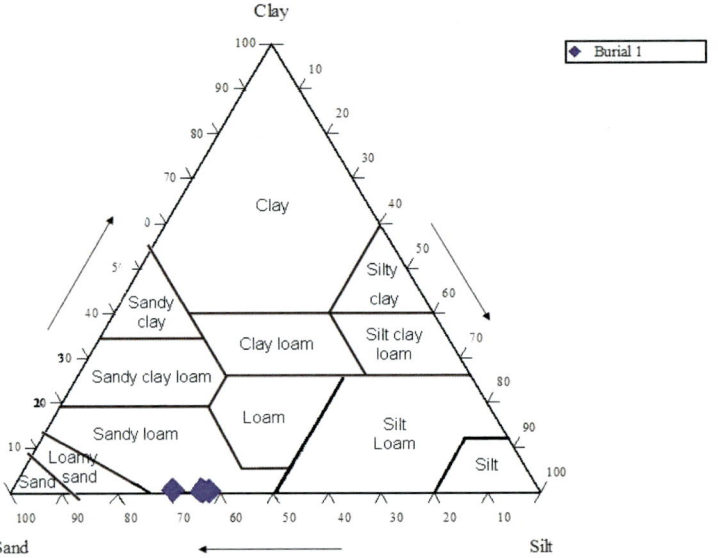

FIGURE 5.1 TRILINEAR DIAGRAM OF SEDIMENTS FROM BURIAL 1

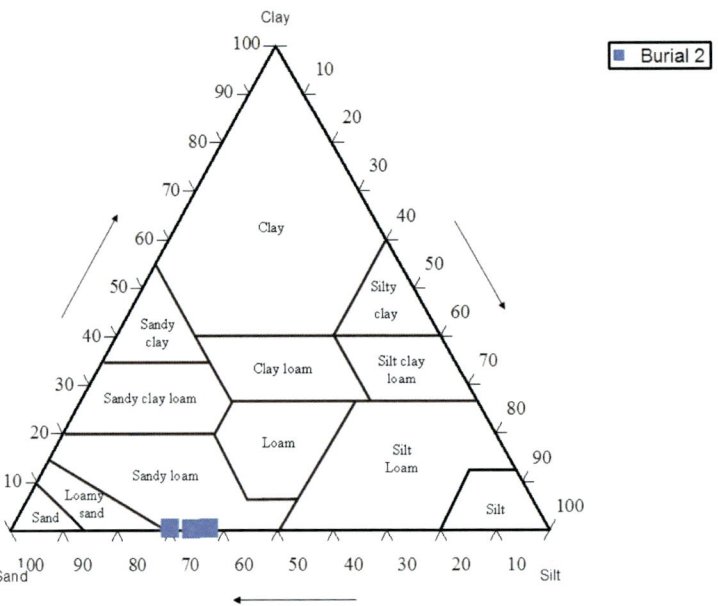

FIGURE 5.2 TRILINEAR DIAGRAM OF SEDIMENTS FROM BURIAL 2

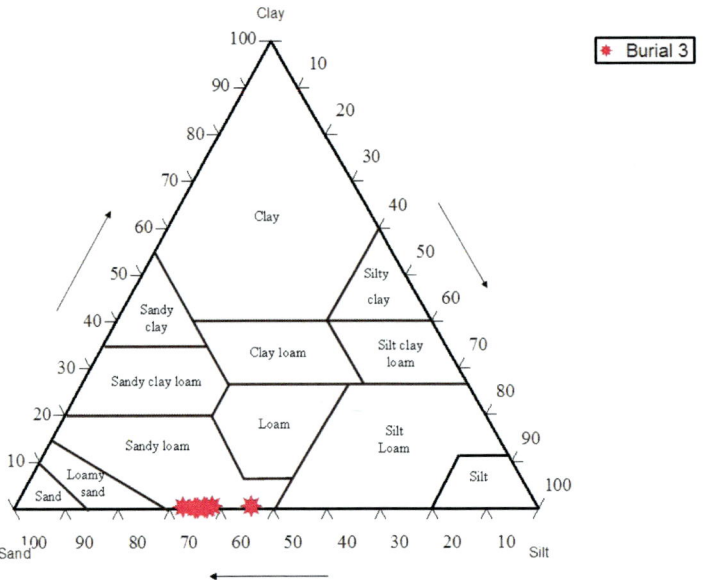

FIGURE 5.3 TRILINEAR DIAGRAM OF SEDIMENTS FROM BURIAL 3

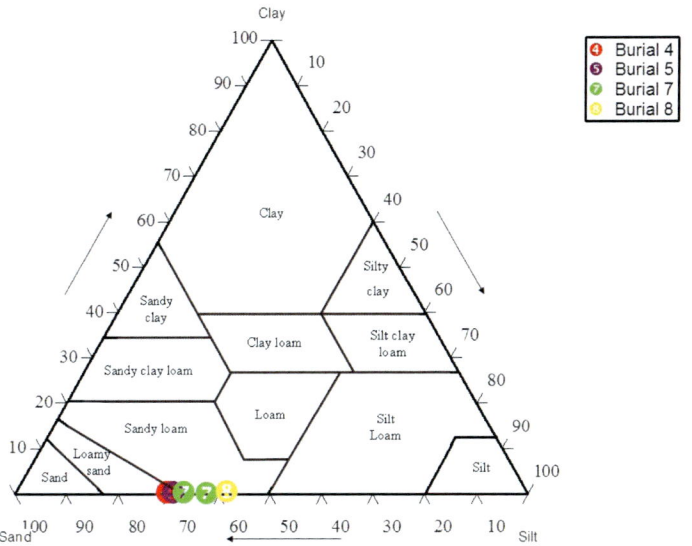

FIGURE 5.4 TRILINEAR DIAGRAM OF SEDIMENTS FROM BURIAL'S 4,5,7 AND 8

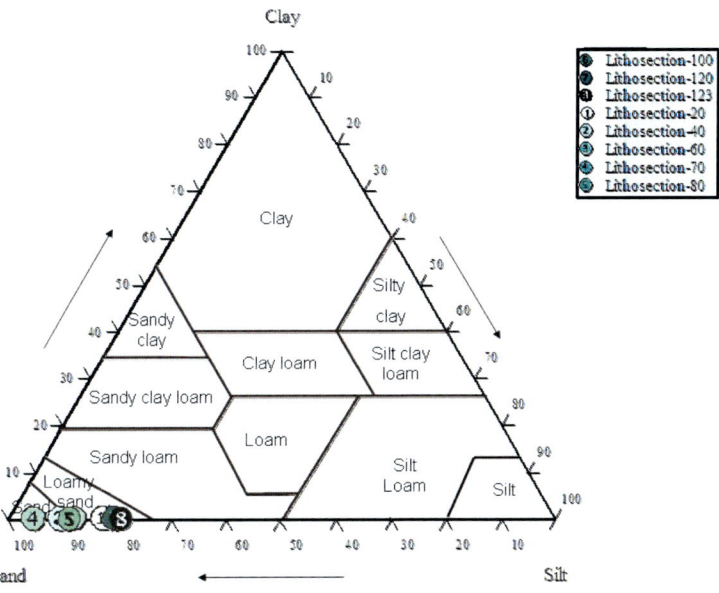

FIGURE 5.5 TRILINEAR DIAGRAM OF SEDIMENTS FROM LITHOSECTION 1

Depth	Mean	Sorting	Skewness	Kurtosis	Mean	Sorting	Skewness	Kurtosis	Sample type
10 cm	0.39	0.99	0.70	3.01	Coarse Sand	Moderately Sorted	Very Fine Skewed	Extremely Leptokurtic	Unimodal, Moderately Sorted
38 cm	0.98	1.39	0.68	0.69	Coarse Sand	Poorly Sorted	Very Fine Skewed	Platykurtic	Trimodal, Poorly Sorted
60 cm	1.67	1.42	-0.12	0.65	Medium Sand	Poorly Sorted	Coarse Skewed	Very Platykurtic	Polymodal, Poorly Sorted

TABLE 5.6 STATISTICALLY ANALYZED SIEVING DATA OF BURIAL 1

Depth	Mean	Sorting	Skewness	Kurtosis	Mean	Sorting	Skewness	Kurtosis	Sample type
22cm	1.70	1.27	-0.10	0.81	Medium Sand	Poorly Sorted	Coarse Skewed	Platykurtic	Trimodal, Poorly Sorted
45cm	2.00	1.13	-0.08	1.00	Fine Sand	Poorly Sorted	Symmetrical	Mesokurtic	Trimodal, Poorly Sorted
65cm	1.83	1.29	-0.10	0.93	Medium Sand	Poorly Sorted	Coarse Skewed	Mesokurtic	Polymodal, Poorly Sorted

TABLE 5.7 STATISTICALLY ANALYZED SIEVING DATA OF BURIAL 2

Depth	Mean	Sorting	Skewness	Kurtosis	Mean	Sorting	Skewness	Kurtosis	Sample Type
60cm	2.021	1.075	-0.018	0.984	Fine Sand	Poorly Sorted	Symmetrical	Mesokurtic	Bimodal, Poorly Sorted
67cm	1.691	1.320	-0.109	0.769	Medium Sand	Poorly Sorted	Coarse Skewed	Platykurtic	Trimodal, Poorly Sorted
70cm	1.940	1.153	-0.060	1.017	Medium Sand	Poorly Sorted	Symmetrical	Mesokurtic	Polymodal, Poorly Sorted
90cm	1.404	1.349	0.029	0.728	Medium Sand	Poorly Sorted	Symmetrical	Platykurtic	Trimodal, Poorly Sorted

TABLE 5.8 STATISTICALLY ANALYZED SIEVING DATA OF BURIAL 3

Burial	Depth	Mean	Sorting	Skewness	Kurtosis	Mean	Sorting	Skewness	Kurtosis	Sample Type
Burial 4	30cm	1.682	1.399	-0.104	0.694	Medium Sand	Poorly Sorted	Coarse Skewed	Platykurtic	Polymodal, Poorly Sorted
Burial 5	35cm	1.539	1.480	0.039	0.585	Medium Sand	Poorly Sorted	Symmetrical	Very Platykurtic	Polymodal, Poorly Sorted
Burial 7	54cm	1.363	1.398	0.170	0.697	Medium Sand	Poorly Sorted	Fine Skewed	Platykurtic	Polymodal, Poorly Sorted
Burial 7	70cm	1.808	1.393	-0.091	0.798	Medium Sand	Poorly Sorted	Symmetrical	Platykurtic	Polymodal, Poorly Sorted
Burial 8	50cm	1.783	1.314	-0.092	0.857	Medium Sand	Poorly Sorted	Symmetrical	Platykurtic	Polymodal, Poorly Sorted

TABLE 5.9 STATISTICALLY ANALYZED SIEVING DATA OF BURIAL'S 4, 5,7 AND 8

5.3 GEOCHEMICAL ANALYSIS OF SEDIMENT SAMPLES FROM SIRUTHAVOOR

The sediment samples collected were also analysed geochemically to understand the provenance and depositional patterns of the burials sediments. While field work and textural analysis indicate reworking of the sediments, the geochemical analysis was conducted to corroborate this data.

5.3.1 Major Element Analysis of Sediment Samples from Siruthavoor

The concentration of Na_2O, K_2O and CaO is very less in all the sediments, indicating removal of the finer particles. The low percentage of Al_2O_3 also compliments this data (Tables 5.11 to 5.15). Low LOI percentage is also noticed in all the sediment samples indicating presence of anhydrous minerals. The CIA index is above 80% for all the sediments also indicative of anhydrous minerals and immature soil.

Description	Depth	Mean	Sorting	Skewness	Kurtosis	Mean	Sorting	Skewness	Kurtosis	Sample type
Section 1	0-20	-0.062	0.583	0.368	2.804	Very Coarse Sand	Moderately Well Sorted	Very Fine Skewed	Very Leptokurtic	Unimodal, Moderately Well Sorted
Section 1	20-40	-0.079	0.501	0.347	2.415	Very Coarse Sand	Moderately Well Sorted	Very Fine Skewed	Very Leptokurtic	Unimodal, Moderately Well Sorted
Section 1	40-60	-0.076	0.517	0.352	2.499	Very Coarse Sand	Moderately Well Sorted	Very Fine Skewed	Very Leptokurtic	Unimodal, Moderately Well Sorted
Section 1	60-70	0.652	1.177	0.697	0.880	Coarse Sand	Poorly Sorted	Very Fine Skewed	Platykurtic	Bimodal, Poorly Sorted
Section 1	70-80	-0.062	0.598	0.373	2.901	Very Coarse Sand	Moderately Well Sorted	Very Fine Skewed	Very Leptokurtic	Unimodal, Moderately Well Sorted
Section 1	80-100	1.354	1.397	0.128	0.656	Medium Sand	Poorly Sorted	Fine Skewed	Very Platykurtic	Trimodal, Poorly Sorted
Section 1	100-120	1.676	1.363	-0.109	0.724	Medium Sand	Poorly Sorted	Coarse Skewed	Platykurtic	Trimodal, Poorly Sorted
Section 1	120-123	1.770	1.332	-0.133	0.800	Medium Sand	Poorly Sorted	Coarse Skewed	Platykurtic	Trimodal, Poorly Sorted

TABLE 5.10 STATISTICALLY ANALYZED SIEVING DATA OF LITHOSECTION 1 1

Depth (cm)	Al_2O_3 (%)	SiO_2 (%)	Na_2O (%)	K_2O (%)	FeO (%)	MgO (%)	CaO (%)	MnO (%)	LOI (%)	Tot (%)
10	8.73	80.74	0.72	0.50	4.35	0.17	0.11	0.07	4.47	99.86
38	9.72	69.90	0.99	0.75	5.15	0.35	0.07	0.32	12.54	99.80
60	10.47	74.66	0.92	0.52	3.56	0.35	0.29	0.12	8.93	99.82

TABLE 5.11 MAJOR ELEMENTAL DATA OF BURIAL 1

Depth (cm)	Al_2O_3 (%)	SiO_2 (%)	Na_2O (%)	K_2O (%)	FeO (%)	MgO (%)	CaO (%)	MnO (%)	LOI (%)	Tot (%)
22cm	5.74	80.90	0.85	0.47	6.84	0.10	0.05	0.07	4.63	99.66
45cm	5.08	79.13	0.94	0.70	8.36	0.15	0.05	0.10	5.28	99.80
65cm	7.07	80.78	1.61	0.63	5.93	0.20	0.05	0.15	3.48	99.90

TABLE 5.12 MAJOR ELEMENTAL DATA OF BURIAL 2

Depth (cm)	Al_2O_3 (%)	SiO_2 (%)	Na_2O (%)	K_2O (%)	FeO (%)	MgO (%)	CaO (%)	MnO (%)	LOI (%)	Tot (%)
60cm	9.80	80.56	0.89	0.56	4.37	0.15	0.11	0.07	3.36	99.87
67cm	6.13	75.89	0.72	0.77	6.36	0.18	0.09	1.02	8.29	99.46
70cm	6.04	82.13	0.62	0.63	4.20	0.14	0.09	0.11	5.84	99.80
90cm	5.61	80.22	3.95	3.36	4.19	0.72	0.31	0.72	1.5	100.65

TABLE 5.13 MAJOR ELEMENTAL DATA OF BURIAL 3

Burial	Depth (cm)	Al$_2$O$_3$ (%)	SiO$_2$ (%)	Na$_2$O (%)	K$_2$O (%)	FeO (%)	MgO (%)	CaO (%)	MnO (%)	LOI (%)	Tot (%)
Burial 4	30cm	7.05	70.17	1.57	1.21	10.89	0.12	0.29	0.08	8.23	99.63
Burial 5	35cm	5.49	82.91	0.54	0.44	4.25	0.09	0.17	0.13	5.8	99.80
Burial 7	54cm	19.15	74.00	1.06	0.71	1.47	0.15	0.15	0.15	3	99.85
Burial 7	70cm	15.21	59.98	1.44	0.93	14.11	0.26	0.21	0.24	7.3	99.70
Burial 8	50cm	6.03	69.17	1.46	0.87	12.05	0.17	0.14	0.08	9.81	99.78

TABLE 5.14 MAJOR ELEMENTAL DATA OF BURIAL 4, 5, 7 AND 8

Depth (cm)	Al$_2$O$_3$ (%)	SiO$_2$ (%)	Na$_2$O (%)	K$_2$O (%)	FeO (%)	MgO (%)	CaO (%)	MnO (%)	LOI (%)	Tot (%)
0-20	6.29	82.18	0.52	0.57	3.91	0.07	0.04	0.05	6.54	100.16
20-40	3.10	82.02	0.69	0.65	10.23	0.07	0.02	0.10	2.17	99.04
40-60	15.45	70.71	0.73	0.58	4.08	0.08	0.04	0.17	6.18	99.69
60-70	13.02	68.16	0.91	0.73	11.88	0.11	0.05	0.23	4.62	99.70
70-80	4.35	85.85	0.62	0.49	4.75	0.06	0.03	0.06	3.27	99.49
80-1.00	5.71	75.56	0.26	0.33	16.52	0.02	0.10	0.05	2.51	101.06
1- 1.20	13.92	70.89	1.21	1.25	5.33	0.14	0.17	0.13	6.48	99.50
1.20-1.23	3.58	86.59	0.57	0.52	4.87	0.10	0.06	0.07	3.03	99.39

TABLE 5.15 MAJOR ELEMENTAL DATA OF LITHOSECTION 1

Depth (cm)	Al$_2$O$_3$	Cao+Na$_2$O	NaO$_2$	K$_2$O	CaO	CIA %
10	8.73	0.82	0.72	0.5	0.10721	86.88
38	6.06	0.9	0.83782	0.6	0.05923	80.16
60	17.27	1.13	0.98665	0.78	0.1428	90.05

TABLE 5.16 MAJOR ELEMENTAL AND CIA DATA OF BURIAL 1

Depth (cm)	Al$_2$O$_3$	Cao+Na$_2$O	NaO$_2$	K$_2$O	CaO	CIA %
22	5.74	0.9	0.85	0.47	0.05	80.65
45	5.08	0.99	0.94	0.7	0.05	74.98
60	7.07	1.66	1.61	0.63	0.05	75.46

TABLE 5.17 MAJOR ELEMENTAL AND CIA DATA OF BURIAL 2

Depth (cm)	Al$_2$O$_3$	Cao+Na$_2$O	NaO$_2$	K$_2$O	CaO	CIA %
60	9.8	1.0	0.89	0.56	0.11	86.28
67	6.13	0.81	0.72	0.77	0.09	79.43
70	10.29	0.13	0.07	0.62	0.06	93.14
90	5.61	4.26	3.95	3.36	0.31	42.42

TABLE 5.18 MAJOR ELEMENTAL AND CIA DATA OF BURIAL 3

Burial	Depth	Al$_2$O$_3$	Cao+Na$_2$O	NaO$_2$	K$_2$O	CaO	CIA %
Burial 4	30cm	7.05	1.86	1.57	1.21	0.29	69.64
Burial 5	35cm	5.49	0.71	0.54	0.44	0.17	82.59
Burial 7	54cm	19.15	1.21	1.06	0.71	0.15	90.88
Burial 7	70cm	15.21	1.64	1.44	0.93	0.21	85.51
Burial 8	50cm	6.03	1.59	1.46	0.87	0.14	71.02

TABLE 5.19 MAJOR ELEMENTAL AND CIA DATA OF BURIAL 4, 5, 7 AND 8

Chapter 5 Results

Description	Depth	Al$_2$O$_3$	Cao+Na$_2$O	NaO$_2$	K$_2$O	CaO	CIA %
Section 1	0-20	6.29	0.56	0.52	0.57	0.04	84.8
Section 1	20-40	3.1	0.71	0.69	0.65	0.02	69.51
Section 1	40-60	15.45	0.77	0.73	0.58	0.04	92
Section 1	60-70	13.02	0.96	0.91	0.73	0.05	88.57
Section 1	70-80	4.35	0.65	0.62	0.49	0.03	79.24
Section 1	80-100	5.71	0.36	0.26	0.33	0.1	89.22
Section 1	100-120	13.92	1.38	1.21	1.25	0.17	84.14
Section 1	120-123	3.58	0.64	0.57	0.52	0.06	75.6
Section 2	80-100	7.08	0.83	0.8	0.55	0.03	83.68
Section 3	30-60	11.52	0.79	0.73	0.51	0.06	89.86

TABLE 5.20 MAJOR ELEMENTAL AND CIA DATA OF LITHOSECTION 1

The graphical representation of the ratios Al$_2$0$_3$/FeO, Si/Al and LOI, CIA, SiO$_2$, Al$_2$0$_3$ (Figure 5.6) indicate a major chemical break around 70-80 cm. This observation is corroborated by the textural analysis and excavation conducted. During exploration and excavation some of the burials were observed to have been trenched as deep as 80-90cm.

5.3.2 Trace metal data of sediment samples from Siruthavoor

Trace metal data (Tables 5.21 to 5.25) and the Cr (ppm) versus Ni (ppm) graph (Figure 5.7) shows that all the sediments fall within the post Archaean region indicating in situ weathering and only localized transportation of sediments. The trace metal data of the sediment samples from the burials vary within the sediments analysed with correlations between depths but also varying from one burial to another. The trace metal data of the burial sediments when compared to that of the lithosection reveal reworking of sediments and local provenance. This view is corroborated due to the fact that if the sediments had been transported from longer distances their trace metal pattern would have been totally different from that of the lithosection. The burials 1 and 2 reveal low content in Co (ppm) when compared to burial 3,4,5,7, 8 and the lithosection also pointing towards the effect of seasonal variation in the Lakes water level.

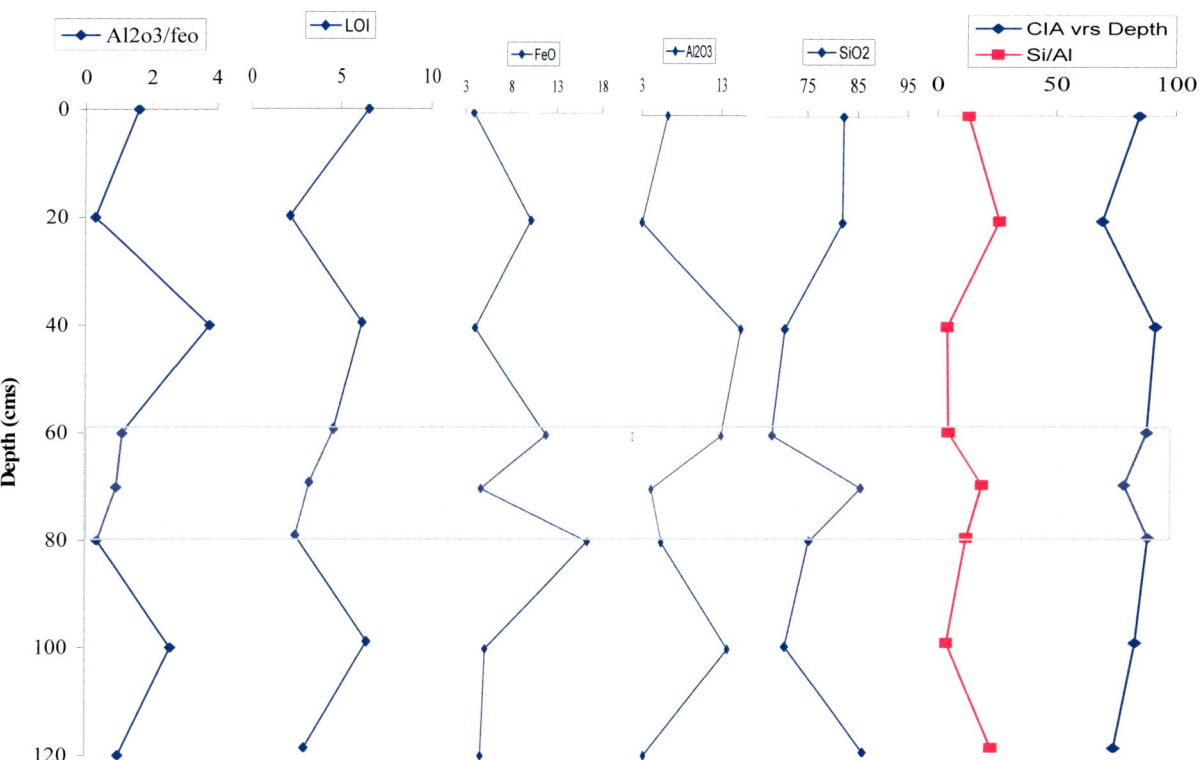

FIGURE 5.6 THE FIGURE REPRESENTS DEPTH (CM) VERSUS RATIOS AL2O3/FEO, SI/AL AND LOI, CIA, SIO2, AL2O3 INDICATING GEOCHEMICAL BREAK BETWEEN 70-80 CM

Depth (cm)	Co ppm	Cr Ppm	Ni ppm	Cu ppm	Zn ppm
10	98.4	142	52.4	76.9	45.1
38	72.6	130.3	39.8	93.9	55.7
60	73	166.6	43.3	113.4	67.8

TABLE 5.21 TRACE METAL DATA OF SEDIMENT SAMPLES OF BURIAL 1

Depth (cm)	Co ppm	Cr ppm	Ni ppm	Cu ppm	Zn ppm
22	37.2	19.4	22.6	64.9	51.4
45	43.3	77.7	42.4	72.9	47.1
65	50.9	67.6	41.5	94.7	54.3

TABLE 5.22 TRACE METAL DATA OF SEDIMENT SAMPLES OF BURIAL 2

Depth (cm)	Co ppm	Cr ppm	Ni ppm	Cu ppm	Zn ppm
60	118.9	124.5	59.6	91	46.3
67	102.3	170.7	65.6	58.4	39.2
70	103.2	166.8	63.2	68.9	40.6
90	118.7	98	65.1	51.6	42.2

TABLE 5.23 TRACE METAL DATA OF SEDIMENT SAMPLES OF BURIAL 3

Burial	Depth (cm)	Co ppm	Cr ppm	Ni ppm	Cu ppm	Zn ppm
Burial 4	30cm	63.1	187.8	39.5	53.7	48.1
Burial 5	35cm	123.7	83.6	50.9	8.2	61.8
Burial 7	54cm	95	115.8	37.1	59.1	46.5
Burial 7	70cm	116.4	124.1	64.2	69.1	58.9
Burial 8	50cm	64.7	149.2	29.6	51.3	33.9

TABLE 5.24 TRACE METAL DATA OF SEDIMENT SAMPLES OF BURIAL 4, 5, 7 AND 8

Description	Depth (cm)	Co ppm	Cr ppm	Ni ppm	Cu ppm	Zn ppm
Section 1	0-20	129.3	139.2	60.7	6.6	85.1
Section 1	20-40	90.8	132.8	40.2	63.6	30
Section 1	40-60	114.2	189.3	63.4	66.6	41.9
Section 1	60-70	115	88.6	55.8	9	28.7
Section 1	70-80	18.7	27.5	156.6	9.6	30.1
Section 1	80-100	104.8	74.2	37.8	9	37.4
Section 1	100-120	122.7	117.6	65.1	9.2	27.9
Section 1	120-123	204.9	77.8	68.1	8.1	38.2

TABLE 5.25 TRACE METAL DATA OF SEDIMENT SAMPLES OF LITHOSECTION 1

5.4 OSL DATING OF POTTERY SAMPLES FROM EXCAVATED BURIALS

Six pot sherds from excavated burials were collected for dating by OSL method and the results are presented in the Table 5.26 below. The dates range from 3rd century BCE to 6th century CE, varying with burial type, indicating long use of this site as a burial complex.

5.5 ANALYSIS OF POTTERY AT SIRUTHAVOOR

The pottery obtained from the excavation at Siruthavoor was badly preserved, making any analysis of the shape and variety of pottery on the site over the period of occupation difficult. However certain features such as Ware and overall quantities did show a pattern. The pottery found at the site include, Black

Sample no.	U (ppm)	Th (ppm)	Potassium K (%)	Moisture Content (%)	Equivalent Dose (E.D.) Gy	Dose rate (Gy/ka)	Age (years)	Date of Burial
Dolman (Burial 4)	2±0.02	13.2±0.13	1.30±0.01	2.15	6.58±0.10	2.81±0.05	2340±51	330±51 BCE
Dolman with circle (Burial 5 C)	1.8±0.02	17.8±0.18	1.85±0.02	2.15	7.32±0.38	3.63±0.05	2015±108	5±108 BCE
Dolman with circle (Burial 5A)	0.4±0.004	34.1±0.34	1.75±0.02	2.15	8.07±0.90	4.38±0.07	1844±208	166±208 CE
Dolmenoid Cist (Burial 6)	0.8±0.01	29.2±0.29	1.39±0.01	2.15	6.27±0.14	3.77±0.06	1664±45	346±45 CE
Urn (Burial 8)	2.1±0.02	18.1±0.18	1.20±0.01	2.15	4.70±0.22	3.09±0.05	1523±74	487±74 CE
Cist with circle (Burial 3)	1.4±0.01	40.3±0.4	1.28±0.01	2.15	6.38±0.08	4.59±0.08	1391±28	619±28 CE

TABLE 5.26 OSL DATES OF POTTERY

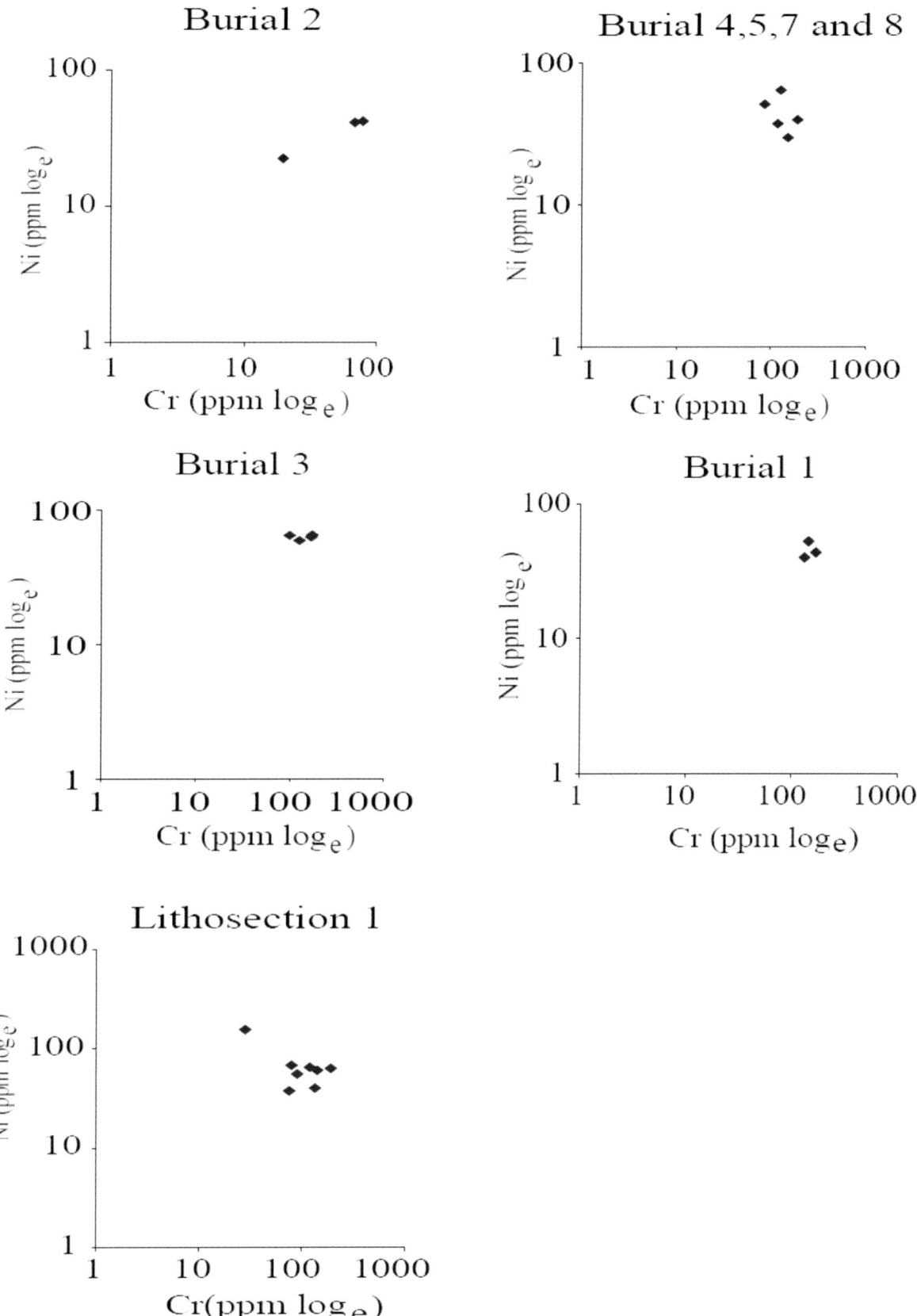

FIGURE 5.7 NI VERSUS CR VALUES OF BURIAL SEDIMENTS AND LITHOSECTION 1 INDICATE LOCAL SOURCE AND POST ARCHAEAN ORIGIN

FIGURE 5.8 RED WARE STAND FROM BURIAL 3 WITH GRAFFITI MARK AT THE BASE

Ware, Red Ware, Black and Red Ware, Burial 3 had the maximum varieties of pottery as well as quantity (Figure 5.8 to 5.10). It had some recurring shapes such as stand, and narrow mouthed pot (Figures 5.8 to 5.10, 5.13). This burial also contained three pot sherds with graffiti, all of which were the same (Figure 5.10). Subsequent analysis showed another pot shard with similar graffiti (Figure 5.13). Black and Red Ware, has been associated with the IA-EH in south India and the production and distribution patterns of this type of pottery has been previously studied (Srivastava 1980). However no proper chronology or understanding of the Black and Red Ware has been reached, though many theories and studies have been carried out, even using the earlier dated Egyptian Black and Red Ware as case studies (Srivastava 1980). Narasimhaiah (1980) believes that the Black and Red Ware manufacturers were a nomadic group of people who spread the production of their Ware through their nomadic lifestyle.

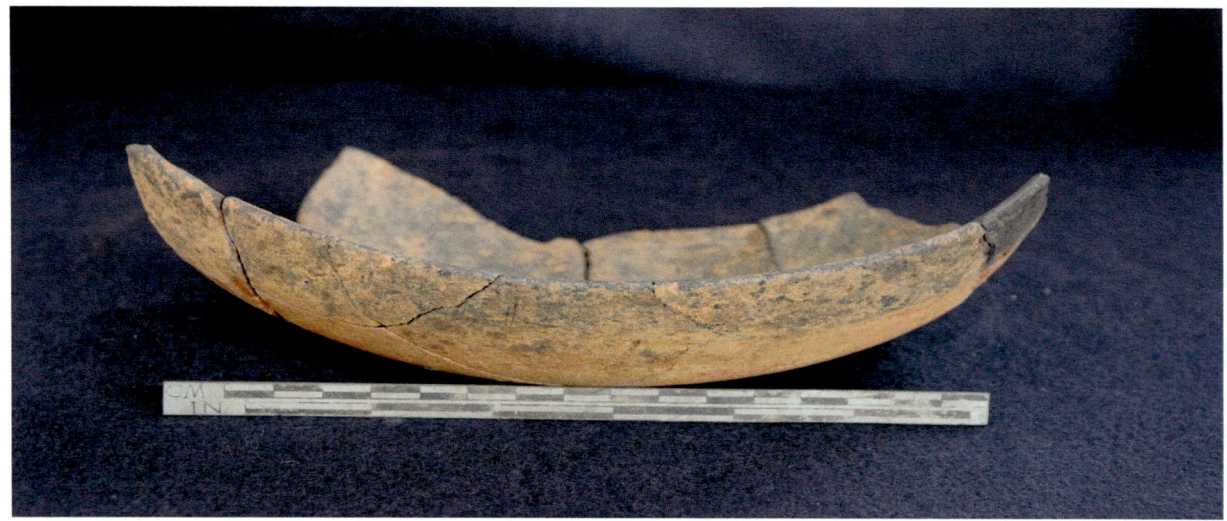

FIGURE 5.9 BLACK AND RED WARE CUP FROM BURIAL 7

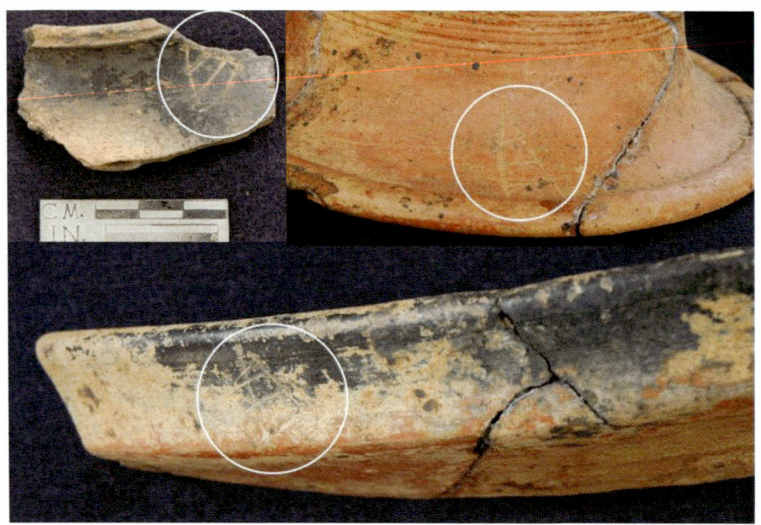

FIGURE 5.10 POTTERY FROM BURIAL 3 SHOWING GRAFFITI MARKS

5.5.1 REE Data

REE analysis was conducted on the pottery and clay samples from Siruthavoor and a present day potter from Chennai (as a control sample) to infer the source of clay used in the making of the pottery at this site. The data reveals that a Eu anomaly appears for both the non clay sample from Siruthavoor and the pottery sample from burial 5 indicating feldspar mineral weathered soil pointing towards a local source (Table 5.27 and 5.78, Figures 5.11 and 5.12). The soil around Siruthavoor is formed over the charnockite bedrock which is rich in plagioclase feldspar and this bedrock also weathers rapidly.

Description	La	Ce	Pr	Nd	Sm	Eu	Gd	Tb	Dy	Ho	Er	Tm	Yb	Lu
Burial 1 25cm	2.21	1.88	1.87	1.93	2.26	2.75	2.16	2.19	2.06	2.07	2.06	2.00	1.74	1.76
A non clay sample from Siruthavoor	0.92	0.85	0.78	0.79	0.85	0.74	0.80	0.79	0.71	0.73	0.77	0.80	0.78	0.81
From Siruthavoor lake	0.82	0.77	0.68	0.70	0.75	0.84	0.73	0.70	0.64	0.63	0.65	0.65	0.60	0.67
Clay Sample 1	0.85	0.62	0.68	0.70	0.78	1.06	0.72	0.67	0.61	0.60	0.62	0.64	0.57	0.59
Valluvar kottam clay	1.16	1.16	1.02	1.05	1.18	1.40	1.11	1.04	0.96	0.93	0.97	0.93	0.86	0.92

TABLE 5.27 REE DATA NORMALIZED USING PAAS VALUES OF CLAY SAMPLES FROM SIRUTHAVOOR AND A PRESENT DAY POTTER FROM CHENNAI

Sample description	La	Ce	Pr	Nd	Sm	Eu	Gd	Tb	Dy	Ho	Er	Tm	Yb	Lu
Burial 8	2.33	1.65	1.93	2.04	2.30	2.76	2.21	2.16	1.99	1.99	2.04	1.90	1.64	1.70
Burial 1	1.02	0.93	0.87	0.89	1.00	1.12	0.98	0.98	0.87	0.87	0.90	0.86	0.84	0.86
Burial 7 Urn	1.64	1.48	1.43	1.50	1.78	2.44	1.65	1.65	1.55	1.56	1.59	1.57	1.43	1.48
Burial 5	2.89	2.31	2.29	2.35	2.51	2.32	2.37	2.21	1.88	1.82	1.86	1.78	1.57	1.50
Burial 7 bowl	1.33	1.26	1.17	1.21	1.43	1.69	1.40	1.39	1.27	1.31	1.29	1.29	1.16	1.22

TABLE 5.28 REE DATA NORMALIZED USING PASS VALUES OF POTTERY SAMPLES FROM BURIALS 1, 5, 7 AND 8

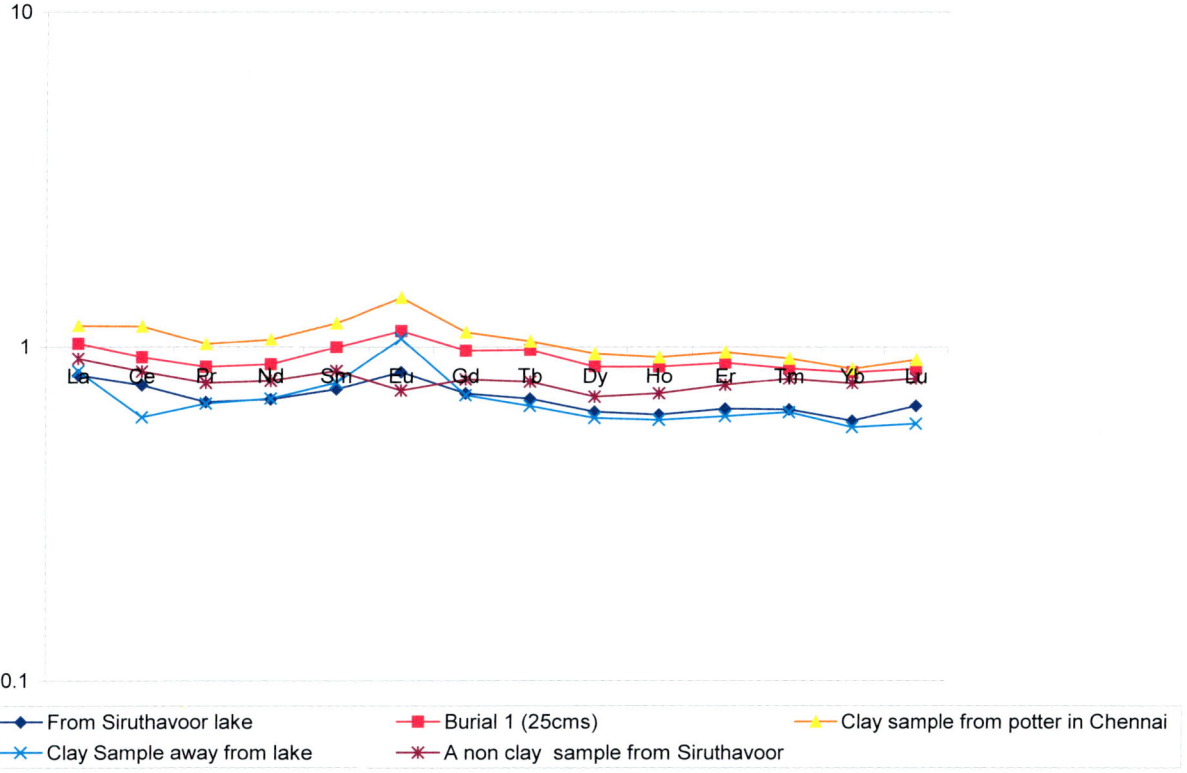

FIGURE 5.11 REE DATA NORMALIZED USING PASS VALUES OF CLAY SAMPLES FROM SIRUTHAVOOR AND A POTTER FROM CHENNAI

5.5.2 Preliminary Examination of Potsherd Thin Sections from Siruthavoor Megalithic Burial Site

Petrographical studies using thin section of archaeological artifacts can be applied to a range of other artifact types in addition to ceramics; including plaster, mortar, mud bricks and lithic implements (Reedy 1994). Such studies are based on the nature of the large inclusions, textural pattern, mineral composition of tempers used, and colour of clay after firing. Groups and evolutionary pattern can also be identified as well as inferring the source of material for pot making. The petrographic analysis of pottery samples show us that the source of clay used for pottery manufacture did not vary much over the 900 years in which the site was occupied. This questions any theory of pastoral nomadic lifestyle, indicating a much more continuous usage of the site

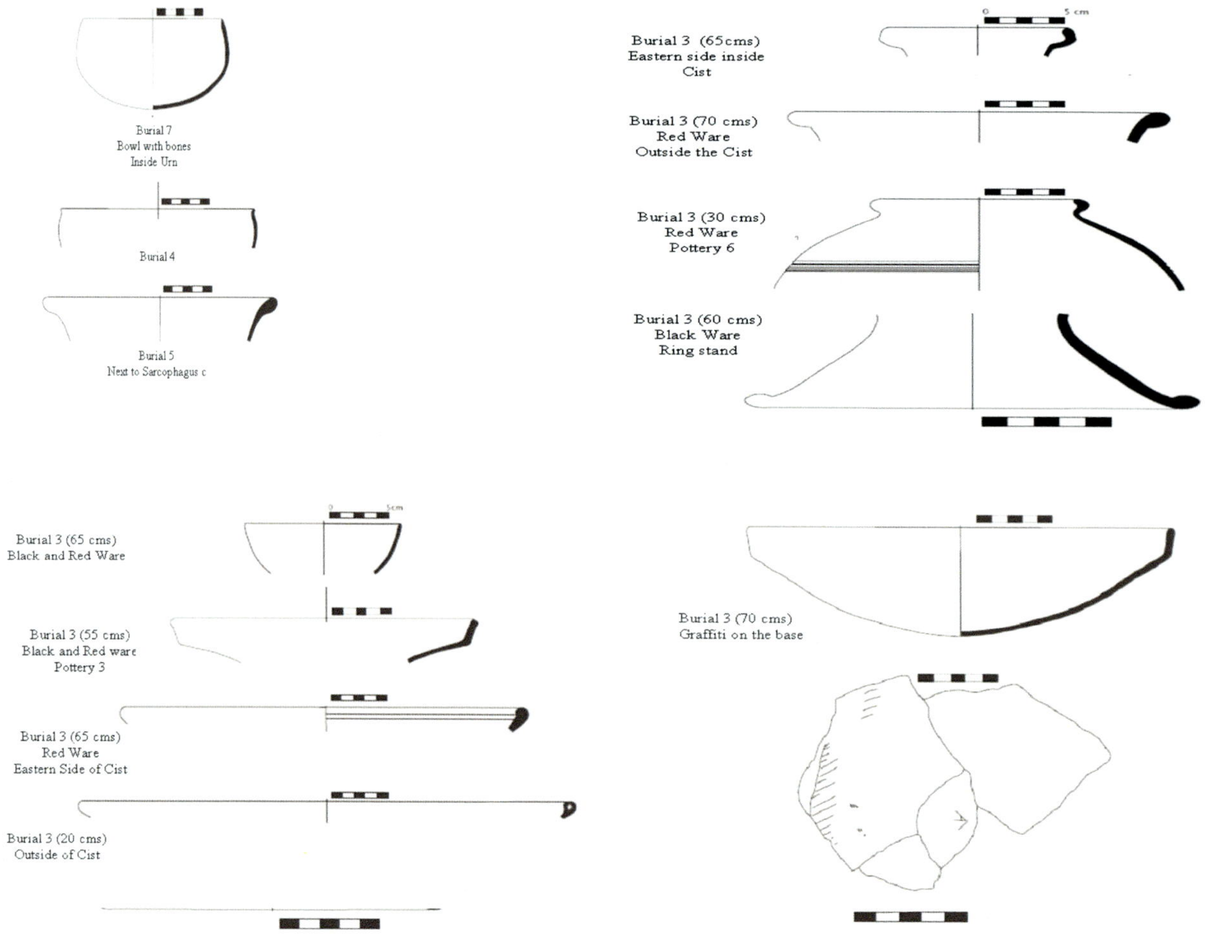

FIGURE 5.12 REE DATA NORMALIZED USING PASS VALUES OF POTTERY SAMPLES FROM BURIALS 1, 5, 7 AND 8

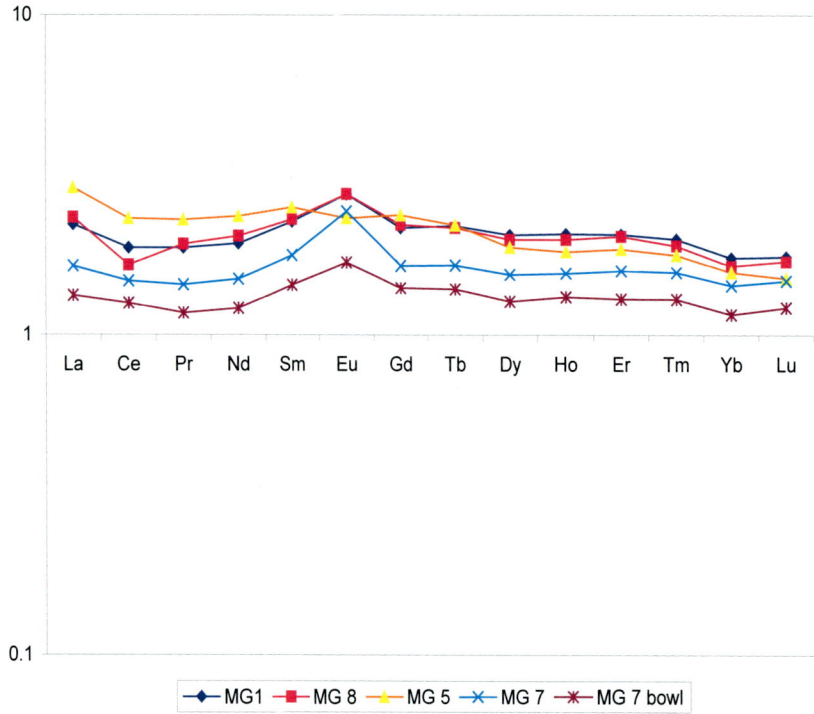

FIGURE 5.13 SHAPES OF VARIOUS POTTERY PIECES FROM SIRUTHAVOOR EXCAVATION

5.5.3 Megascopic Observations

Small pieces measuring ~2 X 2 cm, were cut from each sherds and were subjected to a test in order to determine porosity, mineral composition and texture. For thin section studies pot sherds were collected only from excavated burials. Maximum dimension of potsherd range from 1.5 cm to 10 cm in length with mean thickness of 0.3 to 0.4 cm.

a. The grain sizes range from 80 to 200 μm. Coarse grain size frequency is bimodal, sub angular to sub rounded and stained by iron oxide.
b. Orthoclase feldspar, garnet and muscovite are present and vary from about 5% to 6% in the upper layer to 4 percent in the lower. Some of the muscovite flakes are altered. Coarse charnockite, occur as rock fragments (6-8%).
c. Coarse grains are fractured.
d. It is known that the crystalline structure of kaolin is destroyed at about 600°. The absence of the kaolin group of minerals in the potsherds examined so far indicate that firing temperature would have reached this temperature at least.
e. The crystalline form of quartz undergoes a change at 573°. The fact that the quartz grain in the samples described above is altered makes it clear that, on the whole, maximum temperature could have exceeded 700° at Siruthavoor.
f. Three types of matrix can be identified in the pot sherds (iron oxide, carbonized matrix, and a mixture of both). One of which is composed of iron oxide which may be a mixture of hematite and goethite. Minerals of the iron oxide group in fine grained clay to form pseudo grains which are well rounded and spherical. The ratio of clay matrix to the coarse and fine fraction varies from 6:4 to 8:2. In places the iron oxide matrix exhibits micro fractures and flow structure, alignment of very fine sand grains and traces of cellular structures represent vegetal materials which have been burnt during firing. Pores are in the form of voids-regular to irregular in shape and many times lined with black to grayish very fine silt component or black soot.
g. The analysis carried out renders it possible to determine that the firing temperatures were fairly high. The pottery were fired at high temperature and well baked.
h. The occurrence of very fine charcoal pieces (less than few micron size) in pottery fabric accords well with the non recovery during flotation process. Adding husk to clay for making pottery retains heat for a longer period of time, ensuring less use of fuel.

5.5.4 Microscopic Studies

22 thin sections were prepared and studied under the petrological microscope in detail to trace the provenance of the clay and sediments for making pot. The Siruthavoor potsherds is characterised by the presence of millimetric sub angular to well-rounded fragments of charnockite rock fragments, well rounded coarse quartz, flakes of illite, mica, biotite, plagioclase, K-feldspar and opaque minerals. Occurrence of gorge within some of the pottery samples shows that resource managements were practiced by the pottery makers.

5.5.4.1 Rock fragment and sand temper

Temper sands in potsherds of Siruthavoor include terrigeneous detritus derived from the Archaean charnockite and Miocene sandstone bedrock. Very fine Quartz silt tempers were probably derived exclusively from the weathering of sandstone bedrock. Abundance of orthopyroxene as well as clinopyroxene is diagnostic of charnockite tempers. Mineral composition, iron oxide clay and very fine silt of quartz tempers indicates medium to high grade temperature firing. As regards the presence of these large inclusions in the pottery, petrographic comparison with clay material indicates that the few coarse sedimentary inclusions are natural components of the clay.

5.5.4.2 Iron oxide mineralogy in the clays

Magnetite, hematite, goethite are the dominant iron oxides and clay minerals. Hematite and magnetite represent iron oxide cementing the detritus grains of quartz and feldspar. Iron segregation has produced a great variability of colours, and degree of opacification. Both external and internal colours range from dark red to black, ochreous and brown. Opacification is directly related to the abundance of iron oxides, coal pieces and also MnO_2. An optical microscope was used for the approximate estimation of this abundance (G/M+H ratio). This ratio varies from 7:3 to 2:8. Voids, fractures and channels exhibit laminated clay deposition of hematite and some pores are completely filled by hematite. These fillings have subsequently imparted an overall reddish colour to certain parts of the thin sections. Some of the channels and fractures are also lined with black manganese oxide representing the final filling phase. Very fine carbon are present in iron oxide matrix (Figure 5.14 (a) to (l))

5.5.5 Description of the thin Section

Figure 5.14 a and b. Thin section photomicrograph of the potsherd under the plane polarized light showing specks of carbonized particles with coarse, well rounded to sub angular quartz grains in. **PPL X 50.**

Figure 5.14 c and d. Thin section photomicrograph of the well rounded enriched in iron oxides gorge grains. **PPL X 50.**

Figure 5.14 e and f. Thin section photomicrograph of the well rounded enriched in iron oxide matrix note the orientation of the clay indicating wheel made. **PPL X 50.**

Figure 5.14 g and h. Thin section photomicrograph of the Black Ware pottery (Figure 5.14 g) and Red Ware pottery (Figure 5.14 h). **PPL X 50.**

Figure 5.14 i and j. Thin section photomicrograph of the medium to fine grained potsherds in Black and Red Ware and Red Ware. **PPL X 50.**

Figure 5.14 k and l. Thin section photomicrograph of the soil showing light green coloured pyroxene grains indicating local source (Figure 5.14 k), Figure 5.14 l shows the occurrence of rock fragment in the soil. **BXN X 50.**

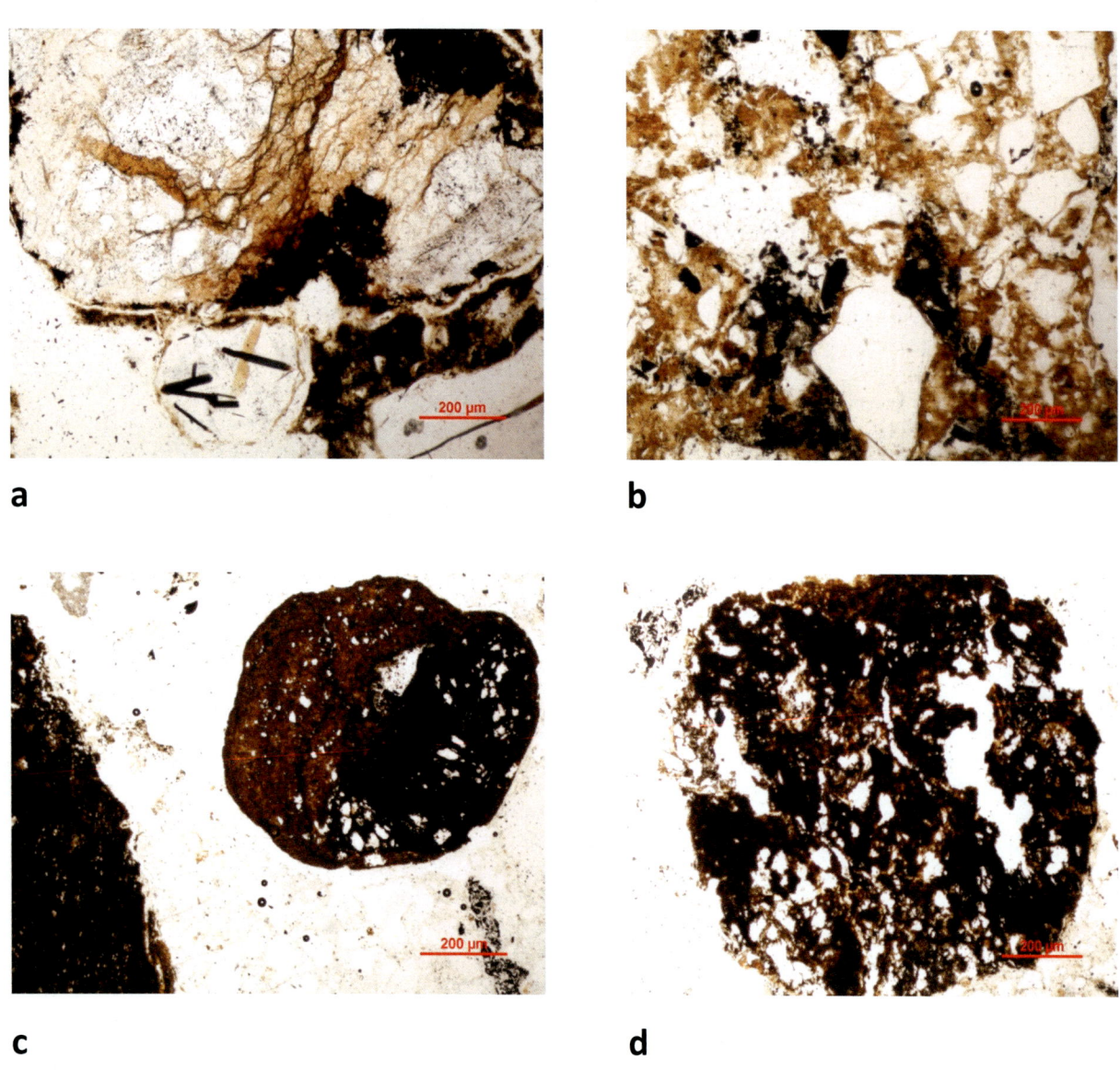

FIGURE 5.14 (A-D) PHOTOMICROGRAPHS OF THE POTSHERD THIN SECTIONS

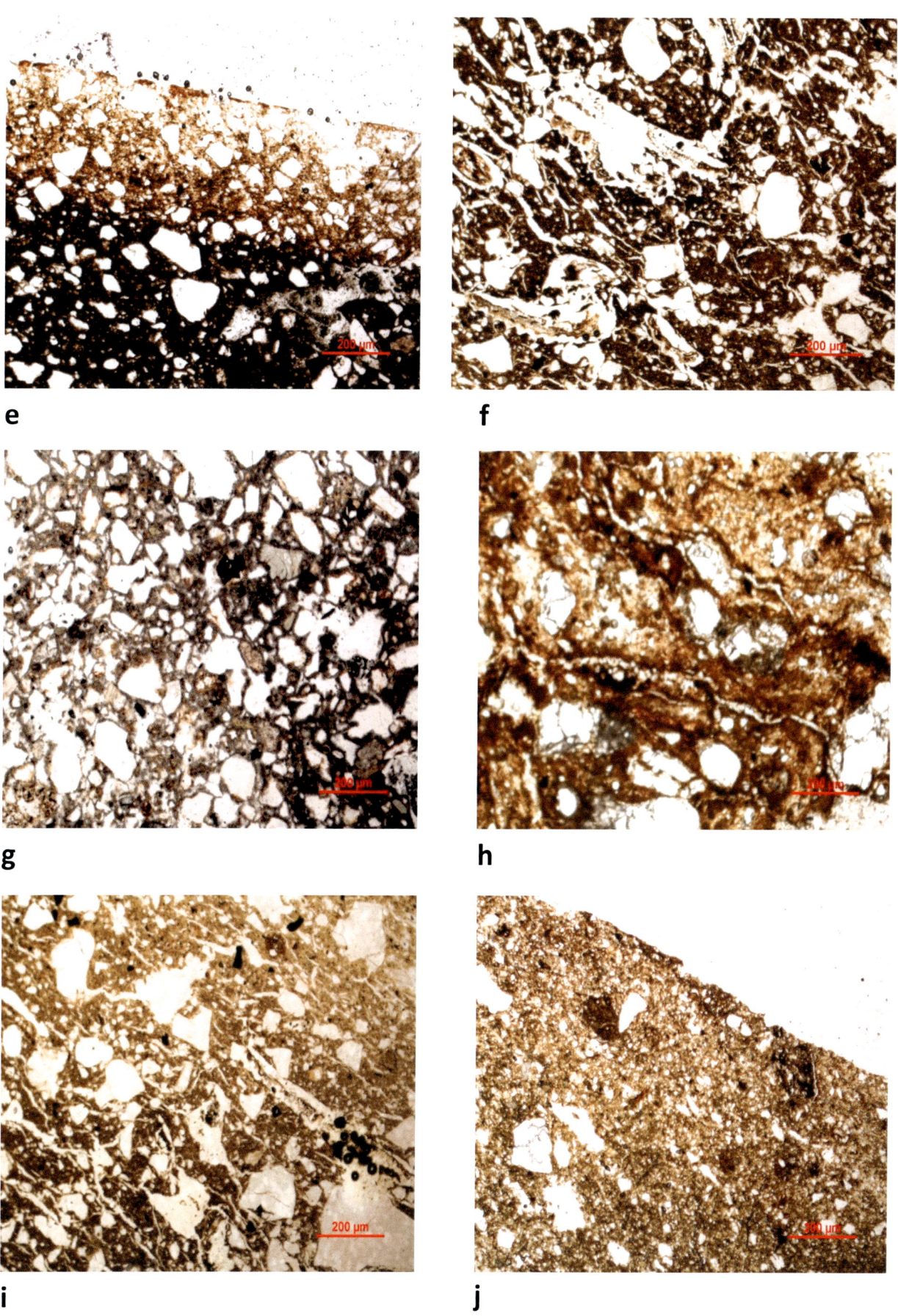

FIGURE 5.14 (E-J) PHOTOMICROGRAPHS OF THE POTSHERD THIN SECTIONS

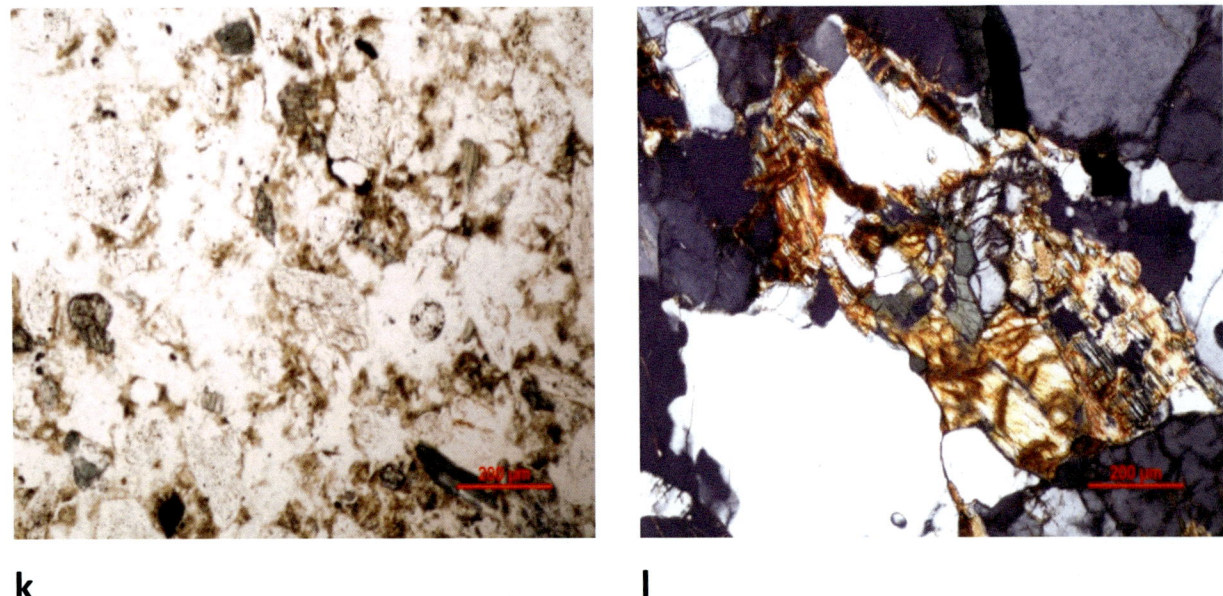

FIGURE 5.14 (K-L) PHOTOMICROGRAPHS OF THE POTSHERD THIN SECTIONS

5.5.6 Discussion of pottery thin section

The sherds are fine to coarse grained in iron oxide matrix. The very fine silt used as temper is heated at very high temperature >800°C as the quartz grain margin are diffused within the iron oxide clay. These finding certainly have important implications for the interpretation of the settlement, as well as the organisation of ceramic production at local source. A preliminary comparison of pot sherds indicates that they are wheel made (preferred orientation of matrix clay and the grains (Figure 15 (i) and (j)).

The results from the sediments collected from excavation of IA-EH burials, as well as a lithosection without any archaeological material show that both sets of sample share a common provenance, derived from the local charnokite bedrock. However while the burials share a common source, they each have certain variations, such as high Co content in burials 1 and 2, as well as burial 1 having more of coarser sediments, due to the seasonal variation in level of the Siruthavoor Lake.

Both textural and geochemical analysis show that the sediments above 80 cm depth are affected by anthropogenic activates, which is corroborated by field data. Analysis of petrography and REE data indicate that the source of raw material for the production of the pottery was locally available, and that while some variations exists within the pottery groups, however the fact that the clay from a pottery in Chennai also gives the same REE results implies that since the region shares a similar source it is difficult to pin point the exact source of raw material. However it is clear that this site has been continuously used in use over a span of 900 years, highlighting the prolonged use of this site.

Chapter 6
Discussion and Conclusion

6.1 INTRODUCTION

With Babington's (1823) early discovery of the 'megalithic' IA-EH tombs along the Kerala coast began the long history of research on megalithic burials in India. Babington was probably not aware that he was opening Pandora's Box for Indian prehistory (Moorti 1994). Since then, for more than one and a half centuries, researchers have been trying to resolve the problems which include understanding how the burials fit into the social context of that period, the chronology and dating of the burials and the significance and classification of typological variations (Moorti 1994). Considering the magnitude of the questions and variation between the megalithic burials, one cannot hope to answer all the questions by studying a single site. This study explores methodologies based on inter disciplinary studies, focused on aspects of the IA-EH burials at this particular site, set within its own regional variations which will lead to the better understanding of how they fit into the larger picture of megalithic burials in Southern India. Leshnik (1974) states that the problems which burials like the megaliths of south India pose can be simplified into three questions, who made them, at what time and in what cultural context. Keeping in mind the landscape alterations that affect classification of burials, using archaeological and geological methods and trying to correlate this with the chronology of IA-EH burials at Siruthavoor are the main objectives of the present study. In order to find out more about the people who built them, the burial site has to studied in the context of its landscape, which in this case is thought to be the Iron Age-Early Historic. This chapter deals with the interpretation and conclusions of the data collected from this body of work. While this work is focused intensely on one site, namely Siruthavoor, the multidimensional quality of the study results in a large amount of data with the potential to create new hypotheses in the study of Tamil Nadu IA-EH landscape and megalithic burials and also to delineate the scope of future work.

6.2 CHRONOLOGY

Barnett (1999) has carried out a study by dating 160 samples to see how the form (18 shards) and fabric (54 shards) correlate with archaeological dating based on pottery and luminescence. The results show a better correlation with form than fabric suggesting that fabric alone is not a good chronological indicator. Megalithic burials in south India have been dated often using Black and Red Ware pottery and iron implements as means of understanding the chronology. Table (1.4) shows that the dates that have been derived for Black and Red Ware sites vary drastically, from Alagankullam which is dated to around cal 399 (368) 109 BCE to Vallam which is dated cal CE 654 (690) 872. This shows that dating based on associated material such as Black and Red Ware or iron implements alone will not help to understand the chronology of IA-EH burials. At Siruthavoor it is seen that the burial 4 dated to 300 BCE as well as burial 3 dated to 600 CE both have Black and Red Ware, Red Ware and Back Ware pottery.

Barnett (1999) revealed that by averaging luminescence ages to obtain higher precision, examination of the relationship between individual features of a site is possible. An analogy can be drawn between the importance of chronology for the Indian megalithic structures and a similar such need identified for the megaliths of the Balearic islands, off the coast of Spain. Gili et al (2006) stated that with respect to the Balearic island megaliths, the different types of monuments arranged in a chronological sequence can contribute immensely towards understanding the relation between the megalithic architecture and the social, economic and ideological changes that took place.

The need for chronological sophistication becomes even greater when one takes an evolutionary approach to the study of the archaeological record (Lipo et al 2005). Chronological clarity with an evolutionary approach is not an allure, in milieu of the megalithic burials of south India contemporarily. However in order to correlate the socio-cultural or economic factors with megalithic burial types as well as integrating them with the landscape to which they belong, chronology is indispensable. Lack of availability of dates for each type of burial within a site makes any study of the different types of megalithic burials ambiguous. Archaeological stratigraphy, radio carbon dates and the study of associated material, dates iron production somewhere along the early 1st or late 2nd millennium, (Possehl and Gullapalli 1999). However the dates from the Siruthavoor excavation reveal a much more complex picture where the IA-EH burials appear to have continued into and beyond the Iron Age of south India.

The megalithic burials cannot be understood completely without removing them from the bracket of not just the term 'megalithic' but also the Iron Age where they have been maintained until now. Each burial site is unique, and needs to be probed and analysed separately before amalgamating the information and attempting to understand the complete picture. The results presented in this study are site specific, but the OSL dates underline the importance of scientific dates for the study of IA-EH culture and also reveal the scope for future work in this area. On the coast of Tamil Nadu, archaeological excavations have revealed that Korkai, Kaveripattinam, Karaikadu, Vasavasamudram and Arikamedu are port sites (Begley 1986). These sites can relatively be dated to the same time period as the IA-EH burials of Siruthavoor. The impact of foreign contact on the eastern coastal plains of Tamil Nadu has been brought to light by Wheeler's and Begley's excavation at Arikamedu, and more recent excavations at Kunnatur, Alagarai and Tirukkambuliyur in Trichy District (Begley 1986, Wheeler 1948, Krishnaswami and Saran 1955-1956, Krishnaswami and Saran 1956-1957, Krishnaswami and Saran 1957-1958, Sridhar 2004, Sridhar 2005). It would be of great interest to discover how the chronological sequence of the megalithic burials relates to the introduction of such elements as writing and the flourishing of early south Indian civilization (Allchin and Allchin 1983).

The results at the Siruthavoor indicate the possibility that certain type of burials such as the dolmens being older than other types such as the cist burials (Table 6.1). The cist burials are dated to 619±28 CE, the urn burials to 487±74 CE and the dolmenoid cists to 346±45 CE. Earlier burials could have been engineered in specific areas, for example around the hillock as seen in the Siruthavoor site, while the more recent ones were positioned further away from the hillock. The spatial analysis also points to some kind of gradual change from the dolmen around the hillock to the cist burials further away from the hillock. However the chronology of the cairn circle type and their spatial segregation from other burial types remains unanswered. It is very tempting to draw immediate chronological sequence and significance to the burials at Siruthavoor from these dates. It is important to keep in mind however, that overlap of burial types in certain areas of Siruthavoor has also been documented. Also the possibility of the continuation of more than one burial type simultaneously complicating any attempts to have any definitive answers, it only gives us a glimpse of the possibilities which such studies could afford.

6.3 EXCAVATION AND EXPLORATION

The variety seen in burials in general, has been attributed to multiple "influences," to freedom of expression, to artistic license, and to colossal bad taste (Trinkaus 1984). Exploration of reported sites around Siruthavoor (Figure 4.1) shows that while not all the elevated rocky regions have been used for the IA-EH burials, all the IA-EH burials in this region are situated in an area with some form of hillock and water body. However the size and type of burials found in each site varies; to understand this more intensive study such as the one conducted at Siruthavoor is required. Rajan et al (2009) have reported that at Thiruporur, as well as Manur and Manamai which are situated in close proximity to each other, there are habitation sites with Rouletted Ware and a IA-EH burail site respectively. Exploration carried out at Siruthavoor, Thiruporur and Manamai reveals that while the three sites have dolmen, cist and cairn circle burials, variations occur in appearance of the different types when comparing the three IA-EH burial sites in detail. Amur, however which is less than 4 kilometers away from Siruthavoor is very similar both in general as well as specific typology to that of Siruthavoor. This implies that the IA-EH burials can be accommodated into previous typological classifications broadly, however with closer inspection and at larger burial sites it is difficult to fit all the burials into the previous system of classifications. Further, sites less than 10 Kms apart have variations, and while geological, topography and availability of raw material need attention, it is not possible to compare and understand the reason for these variations unless each site is mapped in detail.

As detailed earlier, the chronology of cremation and burial, as well as the effect of agriculture, trade and cultural contact is important while studying the IA-EH and megalithic burials. Literary evidence such as *satapatha brahmana*, an early Indian commentary on Vedic ritual as well as accounts of Buddha's death found in the *maha-parinibbana-suttanta* (**t**he Book of the Great Decease), highlight the importance of cremation and fire related death rituals in India (Levin 1930). The lack of any skeletal remains or fragmentary secondary burials found in IA-EH sites, as is seen in Siruthavoor, further raises the question of symbolic burials. A few sediment samples from Siruthavoor were also analysed for traces of Phosphate to verify the lack of skeletal remains and no detectable levels of Phosphate were identified. However the lack of well-preserved artifacts at these excavations also implies that natural factors need to be accounted for before any hypothesis can be proffered.

Research suggests that agricultural practices had become increasingly diversified and intensified during the Iron Age, as evidenced by a wider distribution of domesticates and the construction of reservoirs and other water and soil retention features (Bauer et al 2007). In Denmark, agriculture began around 3100 BCE and the building of truly megalithic monuments began around 2700-2600 BCE, linking the megalithic monuments to the expansion of settlement patterns and the development of agriculture (Kalb 2006). Similarly Sierksma (1963) used ethnographic evidence to relate the development of agriculture with the occurrence of megalithic structures as well as settlement patterns. He also draws attention to differential type of burials with regards to violent deaths. Though Sierksma (1963) and Leshnik (1974) generalize to a large extent on the possibility of a semi nomadic

Burial Type	Age (years)	Date of Burial
Dolman (Burial 4)	2340±51	330±51 BCE
Dolman with circle (Burial 5 C)	2015±108	5±108 BCE
Dolman with circle (Burial 5A)	1844±208	166±208 CE
Dolmenoid Cist (Burial 6)	1664±45	346±45 CE
Urn (Burial 8)	1523±74	487±74 CE
Cist with circle (Burial 3)	1391±28	619±28 CE

TABLE 6.1 DATES FROM EXCAVATED BURIAL POTTERY

lifestyle for the megalithic builders, the co-existence or common usage of megalithic burials by different communities does warrant further study.

The growth of iron in India was a far more complex process than the currently accepted diffusionist position would allow. The earliest site for iron production known from excavated material is from Hallur, having ^{14}C dates of 1000 BCE (Chakrabarti 1977). While the prevalence of megalithic burials is often connected to agriculture and the Iron Age, the date of the onset of Iron Age and agriculture differs around the world (Kostav 2008, Kalb 2006, Sierksma 1963). In viewing the megalithic burials of south India against the background of megalithic burials form other parts of the world the question arises of understanding and investigating the earlier nomenclature. However this research contends that megalithic burials of south India and the megalithic burials around the world share certain aspects, such as their relationship with their landscape. And the use of the IA-EH instead of megalithic in this study is not with the intention of being imperceptive of these aspects.

It would be interesting to juxtapose the beginning of a pluralist society at this period with the results from the exploration at Siruthavoor. The burials here clearly show spatial division between different types (Figures 4.13, 4.18 to 4.22). A near complete typological representation of all the different types of burials existent at the site can be found around the hillock at Siruthavoor. The cist and cist with circles however are concentrated in greater density further south of the hillock as opposed to the dolmen, dolmenoid cist and dolmen with circle which are found nearer the more elevated region of the site. The circles are clearly separated from the other burial types; the reasoning behind this could be social, chronological or availability of raw material and topographic variations.

Trinkaus (1984) states, based on previous studies on the Stonehenge bluestones, that there was no 'long-distance transport' at all of megaliths rather, megalithic monuments were built on sites where the materials for construction were easily available. He further highlights the use of different types of stone for different types of megalithic burials in correlation with their function. He also draws attention to the fact that most of the megaliths in Europe (in the cases of Bulgaria, Great Britain, France and Portugal) show a tendency to be linked to the geological setting of the region. They are built on the place of distribution of quartz-bearing igneous (granites) or metamorphic (gneisses) rocks. While their composition is as a rule of the same rock species, in some exceptional cases rock blocks have been transported from remote areas (Kostov 2008). The megaliths represent the first tendency of humans to build and construct architectural forms imitating the "holy" rock or mountain but the megalithic burials were also a means of finding protection (Kostov 2008).

Chapman (1995) quotes Renfrew's three criteria by which territorial behavior over landscape could be recognized, 1. Simultaneous functioning tombs should exhibit a regular rather than clustered spatial distribution 2. The territories are generated by the activities of the living members of such societies rather than specialized territorial behaviors of cross cutting groups 3. No evidence of social or political hierarchy is present. The literary evidence and study of the skeletal remains from the IA-EH period suggests that there were many cross cultural influences, though their effect on the landscape of the megalithic builders is yet to be clearly understood (Reddy and Reddy 2004, Champakalakshmi 1996, Begley 1983 and Kennedy 1980).

Exploration to discover signs of habitation around the Siruthavoor burial site was undertaken, during which as previously reported, an apsidal Siva temple with inscriptions was located in the present day village of Siruthavoor. Mahalingam (1989) also mentions a Vishnu temple; however exploration revealed a collapsed temple with idols of Subramanya and possible Jain sculpture. Inscriptions on the Vishnu and Siva temples, are dated to 924 CE (regnal year 9 of Rajaraja I) and 994 CE (regnal year 9 of Rajaraja I) respectively (Mahalingam 1989). On the east wall of the mahamandapa of the Siva temple is an inscription dating to 1137 CE (Kulottunga II) in which the name of the village is referred to as Sirudavur or Narasinga chaturvedimangalam. On the south wall is an inscription dating to 1144 CE which records a sale of land made tax free by the assembly (mahasabha) of Sirudavur in Amur *Kottam* to Araiyan Tiruvengambamudaiyan of Ariyalur in Kilay *Kurram*.

As earlier noticed, field work revealed more IA-EH burials to the southwest of Siruthavoor, which is located in the present day village of Amur. Amur *Kottam* is also mentioned on two sides of a slab lying in the courtyard of the Varaha cave temple, the inscription is dated to the 65th year of Nandivarman II, Pallava ruler whose reign is dated to 800 CE (Sastri 1926). Clusters of villages similar to the *nadu* existed within the Pandya and Pallava territory which are referred to in Pallava inscriptions as *Kottam* (Singh 2009). According to Sircar (1966), a *Kottam* was a district within a provenance. In Thondaimandalam (refers to northern Tamil Nadu) the administrative divisions *Kottam* existed prior to the Pallavas and was maintained even after they came to rule (Menakshi 1938).

The temple at Siruthavoor belongs to the 9th Century CE and the use of the *Kottam* implies that that Siruthavoor was inhabited from the pre Pallava period. One of the cist burials (burial 3) from Siruthavoor was dated to the 6th Century CE which means the presence of the burial site and apsidal temple over lapped for some period of time. This lends credence to the existence of a habitation site near the present day Siruthavoor village of an earlier period, associated with the Siruthavoor IA-EH burial site.

Previous reports and satellite data show another possible set of burials at Madyathur. Whether these burials are all of one large site or three individual sites remains an interesting question. The mention of Amur *Kottam* may refer to a different Amur, as the use of the word *Kottam* suggests a larger boundary. The political and administrative boundaries of the Early Historical and Historical periods have a direct impact on the IA-EH burials, rather than those of the present day. It has been hypothesized that the region of Tamil Nadu surrounding Sirthuavoor lingered longer as a pastoralist society, as the Sangam literature does not mention celebrated rulers of this region (Rajan 1993). In further support of this hypothesis, the terrain does not support much agriculture (Rajan et al 2009).

However the extent of the IA-EH site at Siruthavoor and the typological variations indicate that detailed study is required to understand the nature of the underlying society. Wheeler (1948) points out that even after a thousand IA-EH cists have been excavated with utmost care; there will be no significant addition to our knowledge of their chronology. He then highlights the need for placing the IA-EH burials in a related cultural sequence through analysis of adjacent town sites as one of the only ways in which to ensure an advance in our understanding of the older culture. Scientific dating methods, supported by archaeological evidence can probably lead to a better understanding of the chronology of megalithic burials.

6.3.1 Spatial Analysis of IA-EH Burials

Previous work carried out by Wheeler (1948), Rajan (1997) and Darsana (1997) in mapping of megalithic burials at Kodumanal, Brahmagiri and the Upper Palar region respectively, show that burials in these site appear to be separated into groups (Figures 6.1 to 6.7). Out of the six sites explored, two have cairn circles (Ramalai- Darsana 1997, Kodumanal- Rajan 1997) Brahmagiri having cist burials, and the other three have dolmen. Mohanty (1995) at Mahurjhari in Maharashtra also draws similar observations of different groups of burial systems within a single site. Rajan (1994) observes in Mayiladumparai that the burials were influenced by the topography, and that the dolmen were generally found closer to the hillock and cist burials found further away.

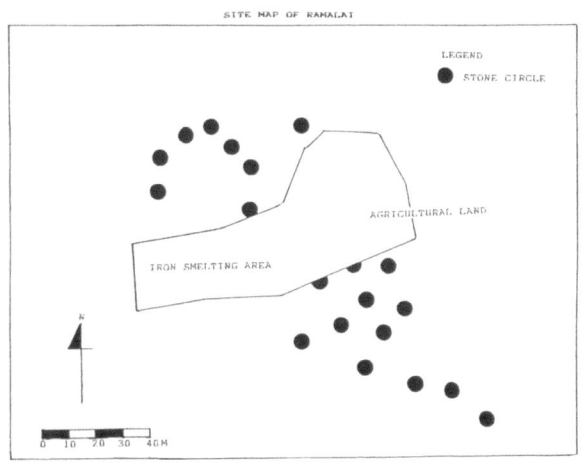

FIGURE 6.1 PLAN OF IA-EH BURIALS AT RAMALAI, IN UPPER PALAR REGION (AFTER DARSHANA 1997)

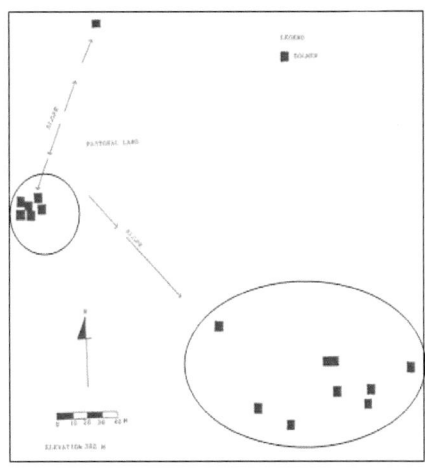

FIGURE 6.2 PLAN OF IA-EH BURIALS AT KARGUR, IN UPPER PALAR REGION (AFTER DARSHANA 1997)

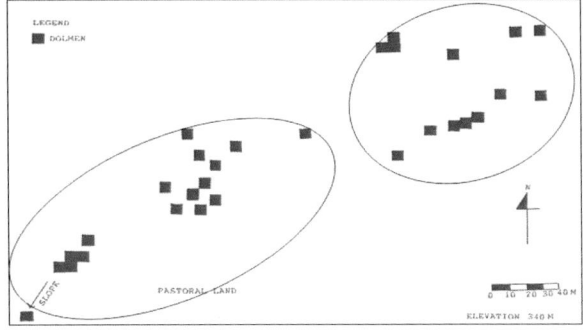

FIGURE 6.3 PLAN OF IA-EH BURIALS AT POGALUR, IN UPPER PALAR REGION (AFTER DARSHANA 1997)

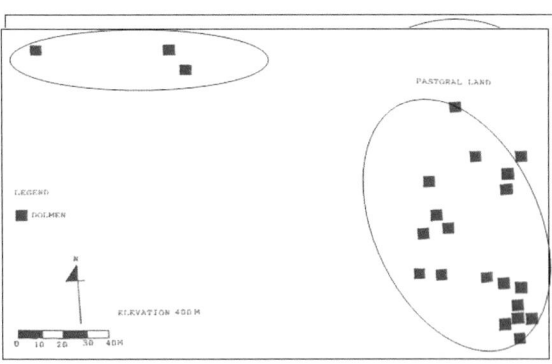

FIGURE 6.4 PLAN OF IA-EH BURIALS AT POONGULAM, IN UPPER PALAR REGION (AFTER DARSHANA 1997)

Chapter 6 Discussion and Conclusion

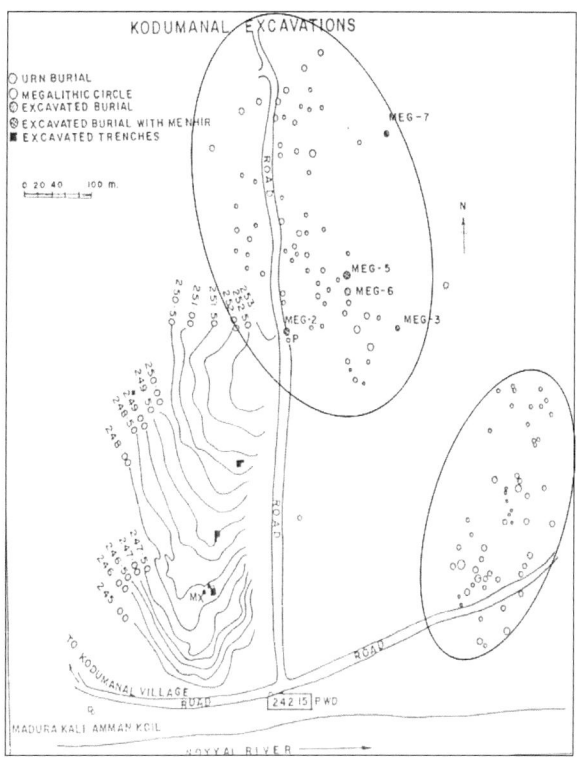

FIGURE 6.5 PLAN OF IA-EH BURIALS OF KODUMANAL (AFTER RAJAN 1997)

The plan of Brahmagiri shows that Wheeler (1948) divided the area into A, B, C and burials from these three areas have been excavated. The overall map of the area shows that areas A, B and C are spatially separate, from each other, and have cist and cist with circle burials. From the map Area C shows that pit with circle and cist and cist with circle burials are interspersed with each other (Figures 6.6 and 6.7). The dotted lines in the plan (Figure 6.67) in Area B indicate a distance of 150 feet which separates the burials into two groups, and; similarly in Area C two distinctly separate groups of burials are noticed. Wheeler (1948) also states that while the burials do have unique features, the construction pattern of all the cists are the same, with a swastika orthostat, which Wheeler states has no special significance but for its functional purpose in holding the cist upright.

It seems clear from the above case studies, that certain divisions of burials were consistently followed. However, not much work has been conducted on analysing spatial pattern of different types of burials within the same site. Whether the above distinct spatial patterning seen at Kodumanal, the sites in upper Palar basin and Brahmagiri have reasons for these divisions, such as topography is not clear. Kodumanal and Brahmagiri have been excavated, and while they explain construction patterns, the correlation between the site topography and its construction pattern, as well as an exploration could help us understand these spatial divisions.

6.3.2 Spatial Analysis of IA-EH Burials at Siruthavoor

Exploration and survey of the burials at Siruthavoor show that the greatest variation in burial types is found around the two hillocks. The smaller of the two hillocks has a lesser density of burials, which may be due to the size of the hillock. However there is a marked concentration of typological variations around the hillock (Figures 4.12 and 4.13). The arrangement of circles (Figure 4.24) nearly overlapping each other as well as the number of burials around the hillock could either be symbolic or due to space being at a premium around the hillock. The placement of a dolmen with circle at the southern end of the hill and two flattened stones appears to add significance to the hillock on the IA-EH burial landscape at this site (Figure 4.30).

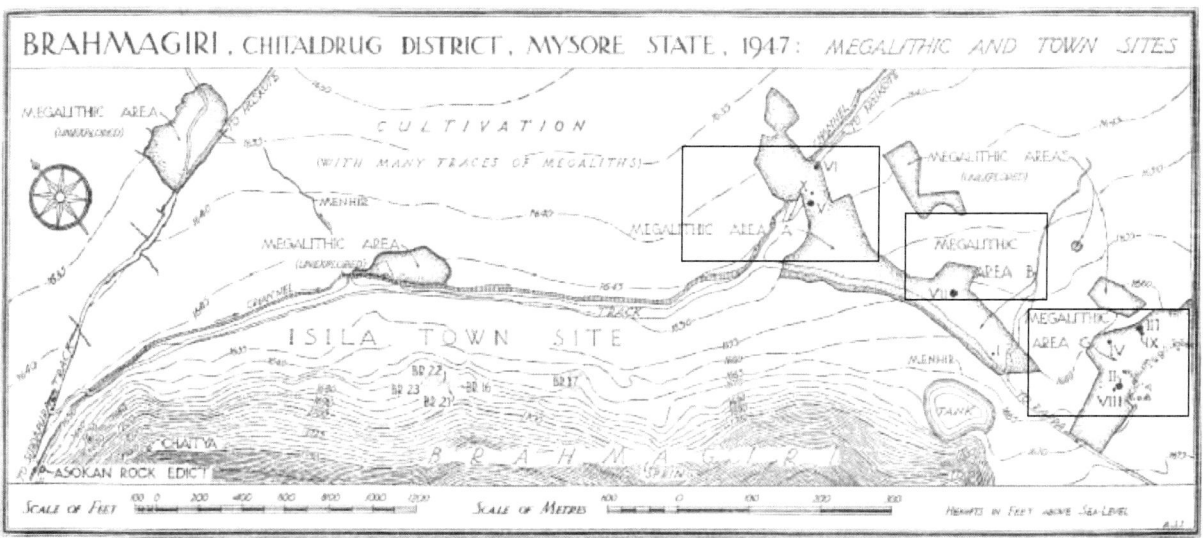

FIGURE 6.6 PLAN OF BRAHMAGIRI, WITH AREA A,B AND C MARKED AND SPATIALLY SEPARATED FROM EACH OTHER (AFTER WHEELER 1948)

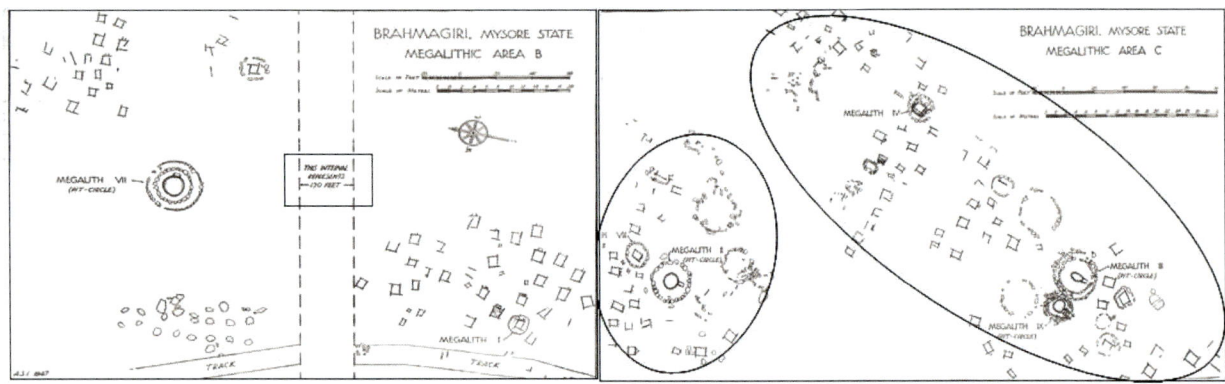

FIGURE 6.7 PLAN OF AREA'S B AND C OF BRAHMAGIRI (AFTER WHEELER 1948)

The dolmen burials with and without circle are the most numerous around the hillock. Previous classifications differentiate dolmen, dolmenoid and cist type of burials based on factors including height of burial above ground, presence of orthostats and whether the material is dressed (Gururaja 1972, Sundara 1979, Narasimhaiah 1980, Allchin and Allchin 1983, Rajan 1991, Rajan 1993, Rajan 1994, Moorti 1994, Krishnaswami 1949 Sundara 1979). However some burials at Siruthavoor do not fit easily into these classifications. The low dolmen found around the hillock with long slabs (Figure 5.27) appears with many variations, and many shapes. They do not have orthostats, to be classified as cist burials, are not low enough to be called a dolmenoid cist and do not have the enclosed space required for classification as dolmen. While some of them have a thin dressed slab on one side of the two long slabs that are the capstone (Figure 6.8 (A) and (B)), others are more rounded and boulder shaped (Figure 6.8 (C,) and (D)). The height of this slab also differs while some are placed well above the ground (height being greater) others are much closer to the present day surface (lower in height) (Figure 6.8 (A) and (C). These variations need more anlaysis in terms of space they occupy within the dolmen burials at Siruthavoor, as well as to understand if the topography, raw material used and construction methods could explain these variations. The type of burials which do fit into classifications are also noticed at Siruthavoor, Burial 4 which was excavated as a dolmenoid cist, though the cap stone was missing, and Burial 3 clearly a cist with the orthostats forming a swastika pattern (Figure 4.49).

However it is the ambiguous burial types which make it difficult to understand megalithic burials, as analysing the features which make it difficult for burials to fit into the nomenclature previously employed are often ignored. Around the hillock at Siruthavoor an aspect that does seem to stand out is the fact that most burials have been partially dressed. A few of the dolmen are made from dressed slabs like those of the cist, while most of them have some features which are dressed while others are left as boulders, without any attempt

FIGURE 6.8 DIFFERENT TYPES OF DOLMEN FROM SIRUTHAVOOR, USING LONG DRESSED AND UNDRESSED SLABS

at shaping the stone. Besides the long slab dolmen, many of the dolmens also have a triangular shaped stone on the eastern side, and a circular base, with most of them having a circle around them like Burial 5 (Figure 4.60).

Around five dolmen at Siruthavoor closely resemble what has previously been described as flush capstone at Oragadur (Richards 1924). At Sanur a similarly described burial has been classified as a cist burial, and unlike those at Oragadur they are separated from the ground by a stone kept below the capstone (Banerjee and Sounder Rajan 1959). The burials at Siruthavoor are similar in appearance but since they have not been excavated their characteristics below the surface are unknown. At Oragadur it was noticed during the excavation of one such burial that underneath the capstone was a pit burial with funereal remains inside (Richards 1924). Clearly there is some ambiguity in terms of classifying of this type of burial, and for the purpose of this survey these were classified as a dolmen. The below the surface features of this burial cannot be seen during any spatial analysis studies conducted, however in terms of differentiation it is an important aspect. It would seem that in trying to fit burial types noticed over the years into previously given nomenclature we are losing information which could otherwise prove important. One of the main aspects of previous studies of megalith burials understood from Siruthavoor is that burial types do not fit into general classification schemes.

The OSL dates of the study reveal that the dolmen and dolmen with circle which were dated are the earliest burials at this site, while the cist is of a more recent date (Table 6.1). Natural factors such as deposition of sediments make it harder to identify cist burials further complicating analysis. However it does appear from exposed sections as well as excavated burials, that the cist type of burial may have spread further south from the hillock towards the Siruthavoor Lake. The OSL date, as well as the large amount of associated material, such as pottery, beads and iron implements excavated and found during exploration as well as the dressed slab implies that these may be of a later date. The difference between a dolmenoid cist and cist type of burial is unclear. Spatially, the dolmenoid cist falls along with the dolmen around the hillock, yet in terms of description of the term and appearance it seems closer to the cist burials (Figure 4.17).

While some cairn circles are found around the hillock their highest density was noticed nearer the lake (Figure 4.18). Due to quarrying activities the burials between the cairn circles near the lake and the cists which are present towards the north of the lake have been destroyed. This is clearly discerned in the map prepared on the distribution pattern of burials at Siruthavoor (Figure 4.13, 4.18, 4.19). Understanding the burial patterning in terms of chronology, topography and associated materials, and the complexity of the burial system makes it much harder to arrive at any conclusive statements. The topography of Siruthavoor (Figure 2.4) shows an undulating surface, and lithologging does show that certain areas have thicker sediment deposition (Figures 4.38 to 4.40).

The dates also show that the dolmen with circle (burial 5) are of a later date when compared to the dolmen (burial 4), and similarly the dolmenoid cist (burial 6) which is without a circle is earlier that the cist with circle (burial 3). The Figure (4.14 to 4.16), attempts a correlation between the spatial pattern of the dolmen with and without circle, the cist with and without circle and the dolmen with circle and cist with circle. The maps show a gradual movement of the dolmen with circle outwards from the immediate centre of the hillock and similarly the cist with circle appear to be in more density further away from the hillock. The area quarried prevents any further conclusions as this area could help define the relationship between the cist and dolmen and those with circles. Comparing the chronology through dates and the spatial pattern of different burial types could prove effective.

6.3.3 Analysis of Data from Excavation at Siruthavoor

From the excavation it is clear that the cist burials yield more artifacts than the other types of burials. Gallon (2008) concludes that the presence of several featureless iron bars (22-60cms in length) in megalithic burials at Brahmagiri (1948) suggests an important association between burial in the higher-social-status context and the possession of bulk unfinished iron. Due to the possible chronological variation between the cist and dolmen burials, as seen from the few samples at Siruthavoor, any parallels drawn towards social hierarchy could prove problematic. However assuming that the dolmen and cist burials are chronologically varied, the cairn circles, need to be dated to understand whether like the urn burials they co existed with the other burial typology. The area within Siruthavoor which is occupied by the cairn circle is not occupied by any other type of burial. The pit excavated in burial 1 was over 70 cms deep, which indicated the soil thickness was enough to feasibly lower an orthostat and yet this area was not used for cist burials. The associated material within the cairn circle as opposed to the cist burials was very sparse. Keeping in mind that reburial could have taken place, and the seasonal flooding of the lake does not create an environment conducive to the preservation of artifacts it is difficult to infer any social or cultural reasons for the segregation of the cairn circles form the other type of burials.

Interestingly out of the eight burials excavated only 1 burial (burial7) contained any skeletal remains. At Chagatur, Mahabubnagar District a few fragmentary skeletal remains and Red Ware in an ashy deposit were exposed while excavating a "dolmenoid cist", that in actuality seems more closely to have resembled a transected cist (IAR 77-78). The report says the site has dolmenoid cists, with or without passage ways and stone circles at the site. This underlies the fact that chronology of burial type, and mode of burial are complex permutation and combinations, and site specific dating and type-wise analysis is imperative for the better understanding of the megalithic burial system.

Moorti (1994) divides the burial types into sepulchral and non sepulchral, wherein the urn burials are classified as sepulchral and the dolmen as non sepulchral. Crookes (1899) theorized that cremation is generally thought to have followed the practice of burying the dead. The dates at Siruthavoor reveal that the urn burials (Burial 8) date around 1523±74 BP while the dolmen burials (Burial 4) dates to 2340±51 BP. This implies that the sepulchral and non sepulchral burials may have co existed, and the chronology needs to be understood in terms of typology as well as social, economic or cultural significance.

Hunt (1924) excavated a cist burial at Raigir and describes that the interior of the cist was relatively hollow, save the silt sediments that had deposited into the cist through the gaps. He states that a study of the exterior of a cist proves that the builders of the cairns intended to prevent stones and earth from entering the cavity. Hunt (1924) also states that the cist was buried in hard soil to a depth of 1.5 feet. Wheeler (1948) also points to the use of porthole cists for depositing skeletal remains as well as other offerings post construction of the burial. At Siruthavoor textural analysis shows that the soil texture of burial 3 includes fine sediments, while the sediments from lithosection 1 are coarser in texture (Figure 5.3 and 5.5, Table 5.8 and 5.10). The cist (Burial 3) does have a porthole, however it is completely filled in with the sediments (Figure 4.57), which do not look to have been post-burial deposition, but rather intentional.

In this case the function of the porthole is vague; however reburial could also explain this aspect. The pottery found within the cist is of more than one layer, and sediment deposits were noticed between the two layers. Which indicates that the possible re-use of this cist burial at Siruthavoor more than once, which can be corroborated from the textural analysis which gives data of alternating mesokurtic and platykurtic which implies the reworking of the sediments (Tables 5.7 and 5.8). If the cist had been filled in only once, then the sediment texture would be more similar rather than alternating.

It is also interesting to note that the burials excavated included a dolmen, dolmen with circle, dolmenoid cist, and a cist with circle burial, altogether showing a chronological movement from 330±51 BCE to 5±108 BCE to 346±45 CE to 619±28 CE respectively (Table 6.1). If analysed with the field survey data, it seems significant that the dolmen were partially dressed, the dolmenoid cist dressed to have a slab like appearance and the cist was well-dressed and had incorporated portholes. This suggests that the dressing of the stone used for construction of the megalithic burial may be significant and needs further study. The survey of dolmen indicates the existence of variations should be analysed in context to the construction pattern.

6.4 SEDIMENT ANALYSIS OF BURIALS AND LITHOSECTION AT SIRUTHAVOOR

The geochemistry of the sediments shows that while the sediments are all from the same source rock, they have been reworked. This correlates well with the survey and dating of pottery, both strengthening the argument that the burials have been incorporated into the landscape using local resources and raw material. The textural analysis and geochemistry also shows a certain amount of localized fluvial activity. When this is contextualized with the field data, the topography (Figure 2.4), the contours noticed on the map (Figure 4.12) and the survey of the burials, it indicates that the external appearance of the burials has been altered over time by erosion and sedimentation. The areas more prone to alteration seem to be the burials closer to the lake, as these are flooded seasonally by the lake, and also affected by the fluvial activity.

6.4.1 Textural Analysis of Burials and Lithosection at Siruthavoor

The negative correlation between the sand and the silt, above 80 cm depth in the lithosection indicates that above this depth some amount of reworking of the sediments has taken place. The trilinear diagram (Figures 5.1 to 5.5) show that the lithosection sediment samples are either sand or loamy sand while all the sediments sieved from the burial are either loamy sand or sandy loam. This indicates that the sediments within the burials have been reworked to a larger extent that those of the lithosection.

The field data also shows that the stratigraphy here is that of a weathering profile. The lithosection 1 exhibits sediments of platykurtic nature of sediments below 80 cm, at which point the weathering bedrock is located. The sediments above 80 cm are largely leptokurtic in nature, supporting the hypothesis of in situ weathering with some reworking of the soil (Table 5.10). The soil above 80 cm is more conducive for burials as these sediments are more weathered. The archaeological burial sediments are all located above 90 cm, and it is noticed that while burial 1,4,5,7 and 8 are platykurtic, burials 2 and 3 are a mixture of mesokurtic and platykurtic, indicating the presence of finer sediments and reworking (Figures 5.6 to 5.10). In the case of burial 3, the sediments alternate between mesokurtic and platykurtic supporting the hypothesis of re-burial. The sediments are also medium to fine textured indicating that these sediments are not a part of the natural stratigraphy and are introduced. Most of the sediments from the burial follow this pattern; however the variability between the burials suggests that the method of filling in of the burials differs, with the requirements of the burial. Field data also suggest that post depositional events affect the appearance of some burial structures more than others. This is further correlated by the sieve analysis which shows that some of the sediments are platykurtic indicating that localized fluvial activity took place.

6.4.2 GEOCHEMICAL ANALYSIS OF BURIAL AND LITHOSECTION 1 SEDIMENTS

The cairn circles closer to the hillock appear to have a very distinct cairn packing (as seen is top left photograph of Figure 6.9) while the cairn circles closer to the lake have no clear cairn packing, except the scattering of small stones around the cairn circle. This can be further explained by the geochemical analysis and the features such as sandy deposit found around the cairn circles near the lake during field survey. The fact that the small stones from the cairn packing remain, but there is no sign of a mound is probably because of the removal of the deposit due to fluvial activity, while the heavier pebbles remain relatively *in situ*.

All the samples analysed for major and trace elements show that the sediments were derived from highly acidic rocks like granite and charnokite. As these rocks are available in this area this data correlates well with the field data. The low amount of Na_2O, K_2O CaO and Al_2O_3 indicate that the soil is residual soil, and after undergoing physiochemical weathering the soil is being locally transported. As the textural analysis indicates this may be due to localised fluvial activity. The low LOI percentage and high CIA percentage is indicative of the presence of anhydrous minerals which show residual *in situ* sand particles. The high CIA index is also indicative of the fact that no intense chemical weathering took place and points towards immature and residual soil.

The geochemical data shows that the sediments within the burials are all local and none of the burials evidence introduction of sediments from elsewhere. The increase in finer sediments also implies the possibility of selective addition of some sediment, either intentionally or otherwise.

The depth at which the bedrock was reached was something to which the IA-EH builders paid attention at Siruthavoor. Some burials may have been placed on the bedrock (burial 4, 5) while others are placed above the weathering bedrock (burial 3). The bedrock weathering in certain areas as seen from lithosections (Figure 4.38) begins at around 80 cm, that the archaeological sediments also extent to this depth is seen from the geochemistry and archaeological data. This shows that the IA-EH builders utilised the topography to suite the needs of the burial type. Whether this shows use of more energy and resources for certain burials, or to suit the available areas of the topography for the purpose of burial is unclear. The sediment data also shows that localized transportation of sediments due to fluvial agents was occurring, implying that certain amount of alteration of the appearance of the burial due to erosion or sedimentation as likely. Thereby presence of cairn packing or height of burials could very likely have changed over a period of time.

Flotation method carried out on sediment samples to retrieve organic remains showed no organic matter or biological remains like carbonized grains, bones and teeth. This points to the fact that the vertisols were not

FIGURE 6.9 DIFFERENT CAIRN CIRCLE BURIALS AT SIRUTHAVOOR LOCATED IN DIFFERENT AREAS OF THE SITE

very conducive for preservation of organic matter. Hence no carbonized botanical remains were recovered that would have helped in inferring the vegetation canopy or agricultural practices of Iron age- Early Historical period. Using these multi and inter disciplinary studies described above, the below conclusions have been drawn.

6.5 CONCLUSIONS

The mapping of the site using satellite data, ground check and field points have revealed that the burials have a distinct spatial pattern. This is clearly illustrated by the density of circle type of burials closer to the lake/ water body towards the Southeast of the site, the dolmen type of burials towards the hillock, and the cist type of burials found in between. OSL dating of the IA-EH burials to 3rd century BCE - 6th century CE has revealed that the dolmen type of burials were of an earlier period than the cist, and the dolmen with the circle was later than the one without (for more on the OSL dating of pottery from Siruthavoor see Haricharan *et al* 2013). Similarly the cist with circle is of a later period than that of the dolmen. Burial 5 had two different sarcophagi sherds, the dates of which are divided by a 100 years, suggesting reuse.

The study also shows that not all the burials at Siruthavoor fit into the prerequisites of traditional classification schemes. It also shows a certain pattern wherein the construction pattern when related to local geology shows a change in types which may have either chronological or social significance. The textural analysis of the sediments shows a larger percentage of sand, of a poorly sorted sample type, implying that there may have been some amount of transportation of sediments through localised fluvial action. This implies that the surface features were altered more by both anthropogenic and natural factors.

The geochemical analysis correlates well with the textural data, indicating an overall common source and stratigraphic sequence for the burials, with certain variations depending on the location of the burial on the site. Burial 1 has a low quantity of Co, which indicates to leeching of trace metal due to the water action of the lake (see Haricharan and Achyuthan 2013). The REE analysis of clay and pottery samples as well as thin section analysis shows that burial type 5, which is of an earlier period than the other samples analysed, has a negative Eu anomaly while all other pottery samples and clay samples have a positive Eu anomaly. However the thin section analysis shows no change in mineral composition of the pottery indicating, local source, long term and continuous usage of the site (for more see Haricharan and Achyuthan 2012). The textual analysis and geochemical analysis of sediments from Siruthavoor show a local provenance of sediment origin with difference in certain regions, due to the geomorphology of the site.

This study shows the scope for future work in applying multi and inter-disciplinary methods to understand megalithic burial sites and their relationship with the landscape. An extension of this study would be to investigate other megalithic burial sites and to see whether they fit into this hypothesis, in terms of spatial distribution and chronology. Understanding the type variations better, with specific references to those burials which do not fit into classifications previously employed. More importance needs to be given to understanding the difference in spatial pattern and associated material for burials which are made of dressed stone and those with undressed stone. More scientific dates are required in order to better understand the chronological significance in accordance with typological variation.

References

Abraham S. (2003), 'Chera, Chola, Pandya: Using archaeological evidence to identify the Tamil Kingdoms of early historical south India' Asian Perspectives, Vol.42, No.2, pp. 207-223.

Achyuthan H. (1996), 'Geomorphic evolution and genesis of laterites around the east coast of Madras, Tamil Nadu, India', Geomorphology, Vol.16. pp. 71-76.

Achyuthan H., Ramasubramaniyam S. and Nagalakshmi T. (2000), 'Formation of Red soils around Chennai , Tamil nadu, India', Indian Geographical Journal, Vol. 75. pp. 17-36.

Agrawal D.P., Kusumgar S., Lal D. and Saran R.P. (1964), 'Tata Institute Radiocarbon Date List II' Radiocarbon, Vol. 6, pp. 226-232.

Ahmad E., (1972), 'Coastal geomorphology of India' Orient Longman, New Delhi, pp.222.

Allchin B. and Allchin R. (1982), 'The rise of civilization in India and Pakistan', Cambridge University Press, London.

Anon (2006), 'Geology and Mineral resources of the state of India', Miscellaneous Publication No. 30. Part VI, Compiled by Operation: Tamil nadu, Kerala and Pondicherry, (Geological Survey of India).

Anon (2007) 'District ground water brochure, Kanchipuram District', Government of India Ministry of Water Resources Available at: http://cgwb.gov.in/District_Profile/TamilNadu/Kancheepuram.pdf [Accessed 18 February 2010], Central Ground Water Board South Eastern Coastal Region Chennai.

Asthana, S.P. 1976. 'History and archaeology of India's contacts with other countries, from earliest times to 300 BC', B.R. Publishing Co., New Delhi.

Babington J. (1823), 'Descriptions of the Pandoo Coolies in Malabar', Transactions of Literary Society of Bombay, London, Vol. 3, pp.324-330.

Badhreenath S. (2011), 'Excavations at Siruthavur', Archaeological Survey of India., New Delhi.

Banerjee N.R. and Soundararajan K.V. (1959), ' Sanur 1950 and 1952: A Megalithic Site in the District Chingleput', Ancient India, Vol. 15, pp. 4-42.

Barnett S.M. (1999) 'Date list 6: Luminescence dates for late Bronze Age and Iron Age pottery assemblages in eastern and northern Britain', Anceint TL, Vol.17, pp.23-40.

Bauer A.M. Johansen P.G. and Bauer R.L. (2007), 'Toward a Political Ecology in Early South India: Preliminary Considerations of the Sociopolitics of Land and Animal Use in the Southern Deccan, Neolithic through Early Historic Periods', Asian Perspectives, Vol. 46 (1) University of Hawaii Press, pp.3-35.

Begley V. (1983), 'Arikamedu Reconsidered', American Journal of Archaeology, Vol.87, No.4, pp.461-481.

Begley V. (1986), 'From Iron Age to Early Historical in South Indian archaeology. In: 'Studies in the Archaeology of India and Pakistan' Jacobsen. J., (Ed.), pp 297-319.

Boivin N., Blench R. and Fuller D.Q. (2009), 'Archeological, Linguistic and historical sources on ancient seafaring: A multidisciplinary approach to the study of early maritime contact and exchange' In 'The Arabian peninsula in the evolution of human populations in Arabia: paleoenvironment, prehistory and genetics' Petraglia M.D. and Rose J.J., (Eds.) pp. 251-277.

Brubaker R.P. (2001), 'Aspects of mortuary variability in the South Indian Iron Age', Bulletin of the Deccan College Post-Graduate and Research Institute, Vol.60-61, pp.253-302.

Brubaker R.P. (2008), 'Regional perspectives on Megalithic landscapes: investigating the socio-political dimensions of Late Prehistoric sites in central Karnataka and west Andhra Pradesh', India Antiquity, Vol.82, p.317.

Bullock P., Federoff N., Jongerius A., Stoops G. and Tursina T. (1985), 'Handbook for soil thin section description', Waine, Wolverhampton, p.152.

Butzer K.W. (1981), 'Rise and Fall of Axum, Ethiopia: A Geo-archaeological Interpretation', American Antiquity, Vol. 46, No. 3, pp. 471-495.

Carver R.E. (1971), 'Procedures in Sedimentary Petrology', Wiley- Interscience, New York, London, p.653.

Chakrabarti D.K. (1977), 'Distribution of Iron Ores and the Archaeological Evidence of Early Iron in India', Journal of the Economic and Social History of the Orient, Vol. 20, No.2, pp.166-184.

Champakalakshmi R. (1996), 'Trade ideology and urbanization of south India 300 B.C. to A.D. 1300', Oxford University Press, New Delhi.

Chapman R. (1995), 'Ten years after: megaliths, mortuary practices and the territorial model' In: 'Regional approaches to mortuary analysis', Beck L.A. (Ed.) Plenum Press, New York, pp.29-36.

Chattopadhyaya U.C. (1996), 'Settlement Pattern and the Spatial Organization of Subsistence and Mortuary Practices in the Mesolithic Ganges Valley, North-Central India', World Archaeology, Vol.27, No.3, pp. 461-476.

Chen S.,Lin B.Z.,Baig M.,Mitra B.,Lopes R.J.,Santos A.M., Magee D.A., Azevedo M., Tarroso P., Sasazaki S., Ostrowski S., Mahgoub O., Chaudhuri T.K., Zhang Y., Costa V., Royo L.J., Goyache F., Luikart G., Boivin N., Fuller D.Q., Mannen H., Bradley D.G. and Beja-Pereira (2010), 'Zebu cattle are an exclusive legacy of the south Asian Neolithic',

Molecular Biology and Evolution Vol.27, No.1, pp. 1-6.

Childe G. (1945), 'Directional changes in funerary practices during 50,000 years', Man, Vol.45, No.3-4, pp.13-19.

Codrington Kde B. (1930), 'Indian Cairn and Urn Burials', Man, pp. 190-196.

Cooney G. (2000), 'Landscapes of Neolithic Ireland', Routledge London, pp.127-128.

Cowan T.M. (1970), 'Megalithic rings: Their design construction', Science, Vol.168, No.3929, pp. 321-325.

Crooke W. (1899), 'Primitive Rites of Disposal of the Dead, with Special Reference to India', The Journal of the Anthropological Institute of Great Britain and Ireland, Vol. 29, No. 3/4, pp. 271-294.

Darsana S.B. (1997), 'Proto historic Investigations in the UppernPalar Basin (Tamil Nadu). Unpublished Ph.D. Dissertation', Pune: University of Poona.

Deo S.B. (1985), 'The megaliths: their culture, ecology, economy and technology', In: Deo S.B. and Paddayya K (Eds.), Recent advances in Indian Archaeology proceedings of the seminar held in Poona in 1983, Deccan College Post- Graduate and Research Institute, pp.89-99.

Dikshit K.N. (1969), 'The origin and distribution of megaliths in Indian', In: "On the problems of megaliths in India", Narain A K and Singh P (Eds.), Banaras Hindu University, Banaras, pp.1-11.

Dixon J.W. (1982). 'Towards an Aesthetic of Early Earth Art', Art Journal Earthworks: Past and Present', Vol.42, No.3, pp.195-199.

Fagri K. (1988), 'The cultural landscape: Past, present and future', In Birks H.H., Birks H.J.B., Kaland P E , Moe D (Eds.) Press syndicate of the University of Cambridge, Cambridge, UK, pp.1-7.

Folk R.L. and Ward W.C. (1957), 'Brazos river Bar, a study in the significance of grain size parameters', Journal Sedimentary Petrology, Vol.27, pp. 3-26.

Fuller D.Q. (2009), 'The Domestication Process and Domestication Rate in Rice: Spikelet Bases from the Lower Yangtze', Science, Vol.323, p.1607.

Fuller D.Q. and Qin L. (2009), 'Water Management and labour in the origins and dispersal of Asian rice', World Archaeology, Vol.4, No.1, pp. 88-111.

Gallon M.D. (2008), ' The political economy of iron in later prehistoric south India', Antiquity, Vol. 82, p.317

Ghosh A. (1989), 'Encyclopedia of Indian Archaeology', Indian Council of Historical Research, Munshiram Manoharlal, New Delhi.

Gili S., Lull V., Mico R., Rihuete C. and Risch R. (2006), 'An island decides: megalithic burial rites on Menorca', Antiquity, Vol.80, No.31, pp.829-842.

Guillore P. (1985), 'Methode de fabrication mecanique et an serie de lames minces', Departmento Sols. Institut National Agronomique, Thiverval, Grignon, p.22.

Gupta S. (2005), 'The Bay of Bengal interaction sphere (1000BC-AD 500)', Indo-Pacific Prehistory Association Bulletin, Vol.3, pp.21-31.

Gurukkal R. (1993), 'Towards the Voice of Dissent: Trajectory of Ideological Transformation in Early South India', Social Scientist, Vol.21, No.1/2, pp. 2-22.

Gururaja Rao B.K. (1972), 'Megalithic Culture in South India', University of Mysore, Mysore.

Haricharan S and Achyuthan H. (2012), 'The Megalithic Burial Potteries of Siruthavoor: Micromorphology' in Multifaceted studies in South Asian Archaeology. S. Rama Krishna Pisipaty (Edt) BAR S2361, Arpitam. Festschrift for Professor Vidula Jayaswal, 107-112

Haricharan S, Achyuthan H and Suresh N. (2013), 'Situating Megalithic burials in the Iron Age-Early Historical landscape of southern India', Antiquity, (87), 1–15

Haricharan S and Achyuthan H. (2013), 'Post depositional processes and the appearance of megalithic burials at Siruthavoor', Indian Journal Of Physical Anthropology and Human Genetics, for a special volume on Indian prehistory and paleoanthropology [Guest editor: Prof. D.K. Bhattacharya] 32(1), 143-162

Haricharan S. and Keerthi N. (2014), 'Can the tinai help understand the Iron Age Early Historic landscape of Tamilnadu?', World Archaeology, 46(5), pp.641-660.

Hart G. (2004), 'Kavya in South India: Old Tamil Cankam Poetry', The Journal of the American Oriental Society, Vol.124, pp.11-15.

Heitzman J. (1997), 'Gifts of power, Lordship in an early Indian state', Oxford University Press, New Delhi.

Herz N. and Garrison E.G. (1998), 'Geological methods for archaeology', Oxford University Press, New York, pp.17-37.

Hill M.H. (1978), 'Dating of Senegambian Megaliths: A Correction', Current Anthropology, Vol. 19, No. 3, pp. 604-605.

Hodder I. (1992), 'Theory and practice in Archaeology', Routledge, London, p. 47.

Hunt E.H. (1924), 'Hyderabad Cairn Burials and their Significance'. The Journal of the Royal Anthropological Institute of Great Britain and Ireland, Vol. 54 pp.140-156.

Indian Archaeology-Review

Indian Archaeology-Review, 1954-55 Gosh A. (Ed.) Delhi 1956, p.55.

Indian Archaeology-Review, 1956-57 Gosh A. (Ed.) Delhi 1957, p.45.

Indian Archaeology-Review, 1965-66 Gosh A. (Ed.) Delhi 1973, p.50.

Indian Archaeology-Review, 1969-70 Lal B.B. (Ed.) Delhi 1973, pp.34-35.

Indian Archaeology-Review, 1970-71 Deshpande M.N. (Ed.) Delhi 1974, pp.32-35.

Indian Archaeology-Review, 1971-72 Deshpande M.N. (Ed.) Delhi 1975, pp.42-43.

Indian Archaeology-Review, 1974-75 Thapar B.K. (Ed.) Delhi 1979, pp.39-42.

Indian Archaeology-Review, 1975-76 Thapar B.K. (Ed.) Delhi 1979, pp.37-38.

Indian Archaeology-Review, 1977-78 Thapar B.K. (Ed.) Delhi 1980, pp.39-40.

Indian Archaeology-Review, 1983-84 Nagarajarao M.S. (Ed.) Delhi 1986, pp.77-81.

Indian Archaeology-Review, 1984-85 Tripathi R.C. (Ed.) Delhi 1987, pp.77-78.

Indian Archaeology-Review, 1985-86 Joshi J.P. (Ed.) Delhi 1990, pp. 54.

Indian Archaeology-Review, 1987-1988 Joshi J.P. (Ed.) Delhi 1993, pp. 102-103.

Indian Archaeology-Review, 1988-89 Tripathi R.C. (Ed.) Delhi 1987, pp. 65.

Indian Archaeology-Review, 1989-90 Mahapatra S.K. (Ed.) Delhi 1994, pp.94-98.

Indian Archaeology-Review, 1992-93 Shankar A (Ed.) Delhi 1997, pp. 88-89.

Indian Archaeology-Review, 1994-95 Dorje H.C. and Banerji A. (Eds.) Delhi 2000, pp.60-65

Indian Archaeology-Review, 1999-2000 Rajeev C.B. (Ed.) Delhi 2005, pp.147-155.

Indian Archaeology-Review,1995-96 Menon K.G. (Ed.) Delhi 2002, pp.71-74

Joussaume, R. (1988), Dolmens for the Dead: Megalith-building throughout the World. Cornell Univ Pr.

Kalb P. (2006), 'Megalith-building, stone transport and territorial markers: evidence from Vale de Rodrigo, évora, south Portugal', Antiquity Vol. 70 No 269, pp. 683-685.

Kallen A. (2000), '*Lao Pako in the late prehistory of mainland southeast Asia*', Indo-Pacific Prehistory Association Bulletin, Vol.3, pp. 93-100.

Kasinathan N. and Majeed A.A. (1996), 'Tirukoyilur excavation', Tamil Nadu State Department of Archaeology, Madras.

Kennedy K.A.R. (1975), 'The Physical Anthropology of the Megalithic-Builders of South India and Sri Lanka', Australian National University Press, Canberra.

Kennedy K.A.R. (1980), 'Prehistoric Skeletal Record of Man in South Asia', Annual Review of Anthropology, Vol. 9, pp. 391-432.

Kostov R.I. (2008), 'Geological and mineralogical background of the megalithic rock-cut sites in Bulgaria and some other European countries', In: 'Geoarchaeology and Archaeomineralogy', Kostov R.I., Gaydarska B. and Gurova M. (Eds.), Proceedings of the International Conference, Sofia, Publishing House "St. Ivan Rilski", Sofia, pp.163-168.

Krishnaswami V.D. (1949), 'Megalithic Types of South India', Ancient India, Vol.5, pp.35-45.

Krishnaswami V.D. and Saran B. (1955-56), 'Excavations at Kunnattur, District Chengleput'. Indian Archaeology-A Review, p.23.

Krishnaswami V.D. and Saran B. (1957-58), 'Excavations at Kunnattur, District Chengleput', Indian Archaeology-A Review, pp. 37-38.

Krishnaswami V.D. and Saran B. (1956-57), 'Excavations at Kunnattur, District Chengleput', Indian Archaeology-A Review, pp. 31-34.

Krumbein W.C. and Pettijohn F.J. (1938), 'Manual of sedimentary petrography', Appleton-Century, New York.

Lawson A. (2001), 'Recent Archaeological Research on Gambian Iron Age Habitation', Nyame Akuma No 55, pp.32-35.

Leshnik L.S. (1974), 'South Indian 'Megalithic' Burials: the Pandukal', Complex. Wiesbaden, Franz Steiner.

Leshnik L.S. (1972), 'Pastoral Nomadism in India and Pakistan', World Archaeology, Vol. 4, pp.150-66.

Levin M. (1930), 'Mummification and Cremation in India', Man, Vol. 30, pp. 29-34.

Lewis A.L. (1916), 'A note on the megalithic monuments ', *Man,* Vol. 16 pp. 26-28.

Lipo C.P., Feathers J.K. and Dunell R.C. (2005) 'Temporal data requirements, luminescence dates and the resolution of chronological structure of late prehistoric deposits in the central Mississippi River Valley', American Antiquity, Vol. 70, No 3, pp.527-544.

Lukacs J.R. (1981), 'Dental pathology and nutrition patterns of south Asian megalithic builders: The evidence from Iron Age Mahurjhari', Proceedings of the American Philosophical Society, Vol.125, No.3, pp. 220-237.

Lukacs J.R. (1990), 'On Hunter-Gatherers and Their Neighbors in Prehistoric India: Contact and Pathology', Current Anthropology, Vol.31, No.2, pp.183-186.

MacKie, E. W. (1977), *The megalith builders*. Phaidon.

Mahalingam T.V. (1989), 'A Topographical List of Inscriptions in the Tamil Nadu and Kerala States;', (Ed.), S. Chand & Company, Delhi ICHR, Vol. 3, pp. 43-47.

Michell, J. (1982), Megalithomania. *Megalithomania.. J. Michell. Thames & Hudson.* pp *168.*

Midgley, Magdalena S., ed. *Antiquarians at the Megaliths*. Archaeopress, 2009.

Minakshi C. (1938), 'Administration and Social Life Under the Pallavas', University of Madras, Madras, p.46.

Misra, V.N. (2001), 'Prehistory of Human Colonization of India', Journal of Bioscience, Vol.26, No.4, p. 491-531.

Mohanty R. (2005), 'Some important Observations: Excavations at Mahurjhari (2001-2004)', Man and Environment, Vol. 30, No.1, pp.106-107.

Mohanty R.K. and Selvakumar V. (2002), 'The Archaeology of the Megaliths in India: 1947-1997', In: 'Indian Archaeology in Retrospect: Prehistory,

Archaeology of South Asia', Settar and Korisettar R. (Eds.), New Delhi. Manohar, Vol. 1, pp.313-481.

Moorti U.S. (1994), '*Megalithic* culture of South India. socioeconomic perspectives', Ganga Kaveri Publication House, Varanasi.

Morrison, K. D., Lycett, M. T., & Trivedi, M. (2008), Megaliths and memory: Excavations at Kadebakele and the Megaliths of Northern Karnataka. South Asian Archaeology, 4-9.

Murray A.S. and Wintle A. G. (2000), 'Luminescence dating of quartz using an improved single-aliquot regenerative-dose protocol', Radiation Measurements, Vol. 32, pp. 57-73.

Narasimhaiah B. (1980), 'Neolithic and Megalithic Cultures of Tamil Nadu', New Delhi, Sundeep Prakashan.

Narayanan M.G.S. (1988), 'The role of peasants in the Early History of Tamilakam in South India', Social Scientist, Vol. 16, No.9, pp.17-34.

Nesbitt H.W. and Young G.M. (1982), 'Early Proterozoic climates and plate motions inferred from major element chemistry of lutites', Nature, Vol. 299, pp.715-717.

Nilakantasastri K.A. (1966), 'A history of south India from prehistoric times to the fall of Vijayanagara', Oxford University Press, Madras.

Pillai S. (1986), 'The Chronology of the Early Tamils. Based on the Synchronistic Tables of their Kings, Chieftains and Poets appearing in the Sangam Literature', Asian Education Services, New Delhi.

Pollard A. M. (2009), 'Measuring the passage of time: achievements and challenges in archaeological dating', In: 'The Oxford Handbook of Archaeology', Cunliffe B., Gosden C and Joyce R.A. (Eds.), pp. 123-139.

Possehl G. L. (1994), 'Radiometric Dates for South Asian Archaeology', University of Pennsylvania: Philadelphia.

Possehl G.L. and Gullapalli P. (1999), 'The early Iron Age in south Asia', In: 'The Archaeo-metallurgy of the Asian old world', Pigott V.C. (Ed.), pp. 153-176.

Premathilake, R., & Seneviratne, S. (2015). Cultural implication based on pollen from the ancient mortuary complex in Sri Lanka. *Journal of Archaeological Science*, 53, pp.559-569.

Rajan K. (1991), 'Archaeology of Dharmapuri District, Tamil Nadu', Man and Environment, Vol.16, No.1, pp.37-52.

Rajan K. (1993), 'Megalithic culture in north Arcot District', Purattatva, Vol.22, pp. 35-47.

Rajan K. (1994), 'Archaeology of Tamil Nadu (Kongu country)', Book Indian publishing company, Delhi.

Rajan K. (1997),'Archaeological Gazetteer of Tamil Nadu', Thanjavur. Manoo Pathipakam.

Rajan K. (2000), 'South Indian Memorial Stones', Manoo Pathippakam, Thanjavur.

Rajan K., Yathees Kumar V. P. and Selvakumar S. (2009), 'Catalogue of Archaeological sites in Tamil Nadu', Heritage India Trust Thanjavur, Vol. 1.

Rajayyan K. (2005), 'Tamil Nadu- A real History', Ratna Publications, Madras.

Rajmohan N. and Elango L. (2005), 'Nutrient Chemistry of Ground Water in an Intensely Irrigated Region of Southern India', Environmental Geology, Vol. 47, pp.820-830.

Raman K.V. (1974), 'Brahmi inscription of Tamil Nadu: A historical assessment', Studies in Indian Epigraphy, Vol.1, pp.104-115.

Rao K.P. (1988), 'Deccan Megaliths', Sundeep Prakash, New Delhi.

Rao S.K. (2007), 'Early man and his culture from Eritrea in Northeast Africa', Indian Journal of Science and Technology, Vol.1, No.2, pp. 1-8.

Rao S.K. and Libseka Y. (2005), 'A Megalithic Circle from Emba Derho: Some Significant Aspects of Culture', International Journal of Ethiopian and Eritrean Studies, Vol. 7, pp. 13-27.

Rapp G.R. and Hill C.L. (2006), 'Geoarchaeology: the earth science approach to archaeological interpretation', Yale University Press, New Haven.

Reddy V.R. (1991), 'Neolithic and Post-Neolithic Cultures', South Asia Books, New Delhi, p. 98.

Reddy V.R. and Chandrasekhar Reddy B.K. (2004), 'Morphometric status of human skeletal remains from Kodumanal, Periyar District, Tamil Nadu', Anthropologist, Vol.6, No.2, pp. 105-112.

Reedy C.L. (1994), 'Thin-Section Petrography in Studies of Cultural Materials', Journal of the American Institute for Conservation, Vol.33, pp. 115-129.

Richards F.J. (1924), 'Note on Some Iron Age Graves at Odugattur, North Arcot District, South India', The Journal of the Royal Anthropological Institute of Great Britain and Ireland, Vol. 54 pp. 157-165.

Rocks D. (2009), 'Ancient Khmer quarrying of Arkose Sandstone for monumental architecture and sculpture', Proceedings of the Third International Congress on Construction History, Vol. 1. pp. 1235-1242.

Sahlqvist L. (2001), 'Territorial Behaviour and Communication in a Ritual Landscape', Geografiska Annaler. Series B, Human Geography, Vol. 83, No.2. pp.79-102.

Sastri K.H. (1926), 'Two statues of Pallava kings and five Pallava inscriptions in a rock cut temple at Mahabalipuram', Memoirs of Archaeological Survey of India, Vol.26, pp.9-11.

Savage S.H. (2001), 'The 2000 Field Season of the Moab Archaeological Resource Survey', In: "Archaeology in Jordan," Savage S., Zamora K. and Keller D. (Eds.), American Journal of Archaeology, Vol. 105, p.3.

Savage S.H. and Dubis E. (2002), 'The Dolmen Field at al-Murayghat, Archeologia', Institute of Archaeology and Ethnology of the Polish Academy of Science, Warsaw.

Sayavongkhamdy T. and Bellwood P. (2000), 'Recent archaeological research in Laos', Indo-Pacific Prehistory Association Bulletin, Vol. 3, pp. 101-111.

Sen P.K. (2002), 'An introduction to the geomorphology of India', Allied publishers Pvt. Ltd., New Delhi, p.40.

Seneviratne S. (1995), 'From Kudi to Nadu: A Suggested Framework for the Study of Pre-State Political Formations in Early Iron Age South India', Sri Nagabhinandanam.

Sesha Iyengar T.R. (1982), 'Dravidian India', Asian Educational Services, New Delhi.

Sherratt A. (1990), 'The Genesis of Megaliths: Monumentality, Ethnicity and Social Complexity in Neolithic North -West Europe', World Archaeology, Vol.22, No.2, pp.147-167.

Shetty A.V. (2003a), 'Excavations at Perur Tamil Nadu', State Department of Archaeology, Chennai.

Shetty A.V. (2003b), 'Excavations at Mangudi, Tamil Nadu', State Department of Archaeology, Chennai.

Sierksma F. (1963), 'Sacred Cairns in Pastoral Cultures', *History of Religions*, Vol. 2, No.2, pp. 227-241.

Singh U. (2009), 'A History of Ancient and Early Medieval India: From the Stone Age to the 12th Century', Pearson Education India, p.594.

Sinopoli C. (2002), 'South Indian Iron Age 361-369', In: 'Encyclopedia of prehistory', Peregrine P. and Ember M. (Eds.) Plenum Publishers, New York.

Sircar D.C. (1966), 'Indian epigraphical glossary', Motilal Banarsidass Publishers, Delhi, p.161.

Sivathamby K. (1974), 'Early South Indian Society and Economy: The Tinai Concept', Social Scientist, Vol.3, No.5, pp. 20-37.

Sjögren, K. G. (2009). Antiquarians at Swedish Megaliths. In *Midgley, M (red): Proceedings of the XV World Congress (Lisbon, 4-9 September 2006). BAR International Series*. Pp 67-78

Smith E. (1915), 'Palestine Archaeology: A note on megalithic monuments', Man, Vol. 92-93, p.163.

Sprangers J.T.C.M. and Balasubramaniyam K. (1978), 'A Phytosociological Analysis of the Tropical Dry Evergreen Forests of Marakkanam, South Eastern India', Tropical Ecology, Vol.19, No. 1, pp.170-192.

Sridhar T.S. (2004), 'Excavations of Archaeological sites in Tamil Nadu (1969-1995)', Tamil Nadu State Department of Archaeology, Chennai.

Sridhar T.S. (2005), 'Alagankulam An ancient Roman port city of Tamil Nadu', Tamil Nadu State Department of Archaeology, Chennai.

Srinivasa Iyengar P.T. (1983), 'History of Tamils- from the earliest times to 600 AD', Asian Educational Services.

Srinivasan K.R. (1946), 'The Megalithic Burials and Urn-fields of South India in the Light of Tamil Literature and Tradition', Ancient India, Vol.2, pp. 9-16.

Srivastava K.M. (1980), 'Community movements in proto historic India', Agam Kala Prakashan, Delhi.

Stein B. (1977), 'Circulation and the Historical Geography of Tamil Country', The Journal of Asian Studies, Vol.37, No.1, pp. 7-26.

Subrahmanian N. (1986), 'History of Tamil Nadu', Selvam Printers, Madurai.

Subramanian K.S. and Selvan T.A. (2001), 'Geology of Tamil Nadu and Pondicherrry', Geological Society of India, Bangalore.

Sundara A. (1979), 'Typology of megaliths in south India', In: 'Essays in Indian Protohistory', Agrawal D.P. and Chakrabarti D.K. (Eds.), B.R. Publishing Co., New Delhi.

Taylor S.R. and McLennan S.H. (1985), 'The ContinentalCrust: Its Composition and Evolution', Blackwell, Oxford. p.312.

Thapar B.K. (1971), 'A Bibliography on Indian Megaliths', State Department of Archaeology, Tamil Nadu, p.14.

Thapar R. (1994), 'Sacrifice, Surplus, and the Soul', History of Religions, Vol. 33, No.4 pp.305-324.

Thom A. (1978), 'The distance between stones in stone rows', Journal Royal Statistical Society, Vol. A141, No.2, pp. 253-257.

Thom A. and Thom A.S. (1978), 'Megalithic remains in Britain and Brittany', Oxford University Publication, New York, p.32.

Tilley C. (1999), 'Metaphor and Material Culture', Blackwell publishers, Oxford, pp. 89-90.

Tilley C. (2004), 'The materiality of stone: explorations in landscape phenomenology', Berg Publishers, Oxford, UK, p.87.

Trefethen J. M. 1950. 'Classification of sediments', American Journal of Science, Vol. 248, pp.55-62.

Trinkaus K.M. (1984), 'Mortuary Ritual and Mortuary Remains', Current Anthropology, Vol.25, No.5. pp. 674-679.

Tripati S. (1993), 'Megaliths off the Coast of Tranquebar', Man and Environment, Vol. 18, No.1, pp.147-150.

Vanamamalai N. (1973), 'Materialist Thought in Early Tamil Literature', Social Scientist, Vol.2, No.4, pp.25-41.

Vanamamalai N. (1975), 'Herostone Worship in Ancient South India', Social Scientist, Vol. 3, No.10, pp.40-46.

Wendorf F. and Schild R. (1998), 'Nabta Playa and Its Role in Northeastern African Prehistory', Journal of Anthropological Archaeology, Vol. 17, pp. 97-123.

Wheeler R.E.M. (1948), 'Brahmagiri and Chandravalli 1947: Megalithic and Other Cultures in the Chitaldrug District, Mysore State', Ancient India, Vol.4, pp.181-310.

Zvelebil K. (1992), 'Campanion Companion studies to the history of Tamil Literature', Jan Gonda, Bertold Spuler, Hartwig Altenmüller, Published by BRILL.